THIS
IS HOW
LOVE
WORKS

THIS IS HOW LOVE WORKS

---

9 Essential Secrets You Need to Know

Steven Carter

M. EVANS AND COMPANY, INC.

New York

M. Evans and Company, Inc.
216 East 49th Street
New York, New York 10017

Library of Congress Cataloging-in-Publication Data

Carter, Steven, 1956–
      This is how love works : 9 essential secrets you need to know / by
   Steven Carter.
         p.   cm.
      ISBN 0-87131-939-X
      1. Love. 2. Interpersonal relations. 3. Intimacy (Psychology). I. Title.
   HQ801 .C295 2001
   306.7—dc21   00-060001

Printed in the United States of America

9 8 7 6 5 4 3 2 1

CONTENTS

for Maggie, in loving memory

ACKNOWLEDGMENTS

A lot of people have helped make this book possible, and I need to give them all my thanks here.

First, my most special thanks to Julia Sokol for generously donating her time and energy to review this material and offer countless ideas, many of which helped shape this book.

My most sincere thanks to George de Kay for supporting this book, to PJ Dempsey for her valuable editorial input, to Rik Lain Schell for his hard work and extraodinary patience, and to the rest of the staff at M. Evans, who are always such a pleasure to work with.

My thanks to my agent, Barbara Lowenstein, and her staff for helping this book find a happy home. Thanks to Peter Coopersmith and the staff at Quidnunc Productions for the website design at **www.HowLoveWorks.com.** Thanks also to Jackie Cantor, Irene Harwood, Frederick Friedel, Ken Sherman, Lloyd Johnson, Norman Haggie, Sonja Eisenberg, Carla Carter, and Susan Hauptman. And a very special thanks to Leonard Post.

So many thanks to the men and women who were willing to share their personal stories in this book so that other couples might benefit.

I need to express my incredible gratitude to all of the authors who have encouraged my work in the recent years, especially Warren Farrell, Iyanla Vanzant, Susan Forward, Howard Halpern, Gwendolyn Goldsby Grant, Linda Stasi, Laura Zigman, Lillian Glass, Ellen Kriedman, and Asa Baber.

Finally, I give my love and thanks to my wife Jill. Without her belief in love and partnership, this book would not have been possible.

INTRODUCTION

I have written this book because I believe in partnership and in the possibility of long-term loving connection. These are not a "given" in *any* relationship; they have to be created and maintained with loving awareness, commitment, and constant work. But they have been the greatest gifts to enter into my life in the last five years—the ultimate "reward" for being completely committed to another human being. In this book I would like to help you experience that same reward.

WHEN PARTNERSHIP WORKS, IT IS NOT AN ACCIDENT

Everyone tells us that it "takes a lot of work" to build a lasting relationship. Rarely, however, do they give us any specifics or concrete information about what that means. When we fall in love, we're filled with enthusiasm; we hope, and trust, that everything is going to work out. What we typically do is rely on the strength of the love and the initial attraction—not "the work"—to see us through. We want to believe that love, combined with healthy instincts and good intentions, will steer us in the right direction. And when we get into trouble, we expect "love" to rescue us. But let's face it, if love was all that was required, many more relationships would "make it."

Through no fault of our own, most of us have not been appropriately trained or conditioned for partnership. It is a sign of the times. Simply put, we haven't had enough practice. Whether we have adored dating and living a single life or loathed every bit of the process, as men and women forming relationships today we have far more skills for being single than we do for being part of a couple.

11

Sometimes we have mastered these "single-life" skills because we had little choice; we were waiting for a love that was slow in coming. Yet ironically these perfected skills are often at the root of our partnership problems. We are too good at being single. We know how to make our own decisions. We know how to make our own plans. We know how to fill in the spaces. We live alone longer and longer, and marry later and later, never imagining that this might make us *less* prepared for serious relationships. In fact, we often believe this will make us *more* ready because we feel healthier and stronger and more self-possessed. But, in truth, we have spent little time honing our *partnership* skills. This is something we quickly discover when that special person we have hoped for does come along, and we find ourselves suddenly struggling with the day-to-day issues of making a relationship successful and happy.

PARTNERSHIP SKILLS ARE LEARNED SKILLS

We all know what it means to fall in love. We know what it feels like to have our spirits lifted by the sense of promise and hope that arises when we meet someone we can genuinely care about. We know how exciting it can be to envision the possibility of a future partnership of two sincere and loving hearts. And we know what it means to invest our belief and hope in that possibility. Yet every single person who wants a loving partnership is wrestling with the unpleasant fact that dreams about love are not always fulfilled. Everyone has gone out on a first date, full of expectation, only to sit across a table from a stranger wondering, "What was I thinking?" Many potential relationships collapse after one or two dates because the initial attraction was simply not enough to carry the couple any further. Some couples manage to stay together for several months, but then the initial attraction wears off, and nothing has arrived to replace it. Some couples are together for several years before the "glue" fails to hold. Many couples get married, and many even stay married—yet how many of these marriages are truly loving and truly gratifying?

Anyone who believes in love, as indeed I do, has to ask the following questions: What can I do to ensure the success of my relationship? What can I do each day to make my relationship more loving and fulfilling? How can I make sure that my partner and I will continue to connect and grow together?

In the twenty years I have been studying, observing, and writing about romantic relationships, I am constantly surprised by the number of people who tell me that even though they think they have found the partner of their dreams, they are failing to create the relationship they expected. These men and women insist they have all the "basics": love, real chemistry, good intentions, shared interests, shared values, shared goals, and a willingness to work on the relationship. Many are quick to point out that they have great sex. And I believe all of their claims. Regardless of what they *do* have, however, they do not feel satisfied. The relationship isn't taking care of their needs. Something is wrong, but they don't know what that "something" is.

Yet some relationships *do* thrive. The partners start off loving and hopeful, *and* they continue that way. Strong, healthy, resilient bonds develop; the relationship grows and flourishes; and both partners feel satisfied and connected. What do the women and men in these relationships know? What do they do that is different? What keeps these connections so vital?

WE NEED BLUEPRINTS TO BUILD RELATIONSHIP BRIDGES

When I finally met the woman I was eventually to marry, my need for very precise information about what truly works and what doesn't became much more urgent. I had a wonderful partner, but like most people, I had no real relationship blueprints in my head. I didn't know how to make the bridge from a promising beginning to a never-ending story. This wasn't a professional exploration. "This time," as they say in the movies, "it was personal." I wanted my relationship to work. And though I wanted to believe that the strength of our attraction and the strength of our commitment was enough to weather any storm, the more sensible side of me already knew better. When you are riding the coattails of your initial connection, it doesn't take long before those coattails show their wear. Great beginnings are only great beginnings.

As someone who writes books that explore the subject of romantic relationships, I know it's not enough to say "You have to communicate" or "You have to embrace differences" or "It's a Mars-Venus problem." Relationships are far more complicated than that. I also know that if you are going to make it through days, months, and years of relationship challenges, your instincts—however healthy—and your loving heart—however strong—are not always enough. When you are trying to get someplace you have never been before, it makes a huge difference to see the footprints of others in front of you. When you are building something you have never successfully built before, you wouldn't get started without a clear set of blueprints. Yet that is something we do in our personal lives all the time: We take steps into the future with our partners, having no clear idea if these are the steps that will lead us to our goals.

For years I have written books about relationship struggles—how to make good choices, how to avoid common pitfalls, how to be more self-protective, how to deal with fears and open the doors to commitment. Nonetheless, it was clear to me from the beginning that my own instincts and intuition—valuable though they were—were not going to provide me with all the answers. It is one thing to have a clear understanding of relationship dynamics; it is quite another to feel grounded in partnership skills. The latter requires many more years of *personal* experience in a successful partnership, and I couldn't trust that my own limited experiences were going to give me all the answers. On more than one occasion I found myself turning to close friends and crying, "Help!" In many ways, I felt as though I was starting from the beginning in a very new and different world. Like so many individuals who are sincerely trying to build their first solid bridge from "me" to "we," I needed new information—information that is embedded in the experiences of successful couples.

Notebook in hand, I started a long and detailed exploration of the partnership experience—an experience that only looks simple when you are doing it exactly right. I reviewed old interviews with couples I had spoken to over the past fifteen years, trying to see them with new eyes. Then I began talking to more couples—young, old, and in between. Some of these were couples whose relationships I admired; others were couples whose relationships I feared. I searched for role models whose successes could be duplicated, and I was also careful to catalogue mistakes or missteps.

For me, this experience was both fascinating and humbling. It was humbling because I had to become a student again, and step down from that all-too-comfortable "relationship expert" pedestal. It was fascinating because these couples gave me so much new information. Some successful couples were aware of all the "work" they were putting into their partnerships; they were able to artfully articulate what that process entailed. Other couples seemed to have a more natural affinity for "getting it right" and were surprised by my admiration for a process they took so much for granted. But everywhere I turned, there was something new to be learned.

Having lived for so long as a single man in an uncoupled world, I was constantly surprised by what I was discovering. And what fascinated me most was the slow but clear emergence of nine separate and distinct principles that seemed to govern the day-to-day interaction of people who are truly happy with each other. These essential rules for behavior were not at all obvious at first, which is why I like to call them "secrets." We can easily overlook many of them because they are so delicately woven into the fabric of a successful relationship, and it actually took almost three years before I was able to see all nine secrets clearly. But once I could see them all, my entire understanding of relationships changed dramatically. I don't doubt that you will have a similar experience.

A PRACTICAL FRAMEWORK FOR MAKING LOVE WORK

When it comes to relationships, I have never been a big believer in "rules and regulations," and those readers who are familiar with my work already know that. Relationships are a fluid process, and trying to control that process with too many "musts" and "shoulds" can easily turn a potentially happy couple into a very unhappy stereotype.

On the other hand, it isn't hard to understand why men and women are often comforted by someone else's relationship rules and regulations. Let's face it, even the best relationships can be confusing and difficult. Times have changed, and this has changed our relationships, leaving people yearning for "the good old days" when relationship behaviors were clearly scripted. It can feel like an emotional jungle out there, and it can be so hard to walk through that jungle. But most of the "jungle" rules and regulations being offered today tend to encourage manipulation and control, and discourage individuality, openness, flexibility, and experimentation. This is why most relationship "rules" ultimately fail.

The nine essential secrets presented in the pages that follow are very different. These guidelines are not ephemeral, ungraspable, inflexible, or manipulative. They are not exhausting, intimidating, or hopelessly complex. To the contrary, they are easily understood, and easily put into daily practice. Some of them you may be following naturally right now, without fully understanding why; others can be incorporated with little effort. Awareness is the key. And that is what this book is all about.

Introduction

We all know that relationships are challenging. These days, they seem harder than ever. It takes so much work to build and maintain something vital, and so much *less* work to walk away. But let's face it: Life is, more than anything, about love and connection—connection with friends, with family, and, if we are truly lucky, with a special partner. My partnership with my wife Jill has changed my life comprehensively, in every positive way. And it is the kind of partnership I wish for you. This hasn't been easy for us, but it hasn't been impossible either. We have both learned that when you are following a clear set of healthy blueprints, you just need to keep putting one foot in front of the other. I call these blueprints my "nine essential secrets." You can call them anything you like, as long as you commit them to memory and follow them with your head and heart.

· ◆ ·

In his unforgettable film *Annie Hall,* Woody Allen told his audience that a relationship is like a shark—if it doesn't keep moving forward, it dies. We laughed at the image, but we also recognized some piece of truth in it. Relationships *are* always moving. Either they are moving forward in the direction of stronger partnership, or they are losing ground. There is no magical still point; there is no way to put even the most powerful love in neutral and coast for a while. This is why relationships can be so challenging. And it is why love and attraction are not always enough to keep two partners happy with each other.

Perhaps "love" itself—its origins, and its power—will always be a mystery. Why a relationship works or doesn't work, however, is *not* a total mystery. It is only a challenge that you can easily meet if you have the tools. The nine essential secrets you will read about in this book are those very tools—tools that keep a relationship energized, on the right track, and constantly moving forward in the right direction. They create a simple framework for what we all want most— lasting, loving partnership.

SECRET #1:

Notice the Small Stuff

• ◆ •

I can get pretty annoyed when I hear people taking the popular axiom, "Don't sweat the small stuff," and dispensing it as *relationship* advice to their friends, their partners, or themselves. *In the world of love and relationships, there is no such thing as "too small to be important."* Every single issue can have an impact, every single gesture carries some weight. Relationships provide a constant stream of "small stuff" where every piece can make a difference. These small pieces, when they are negative, can collect very quickly into large problems—sometimes even deal-breaking problems. Conversely, an ongoing supply of small positive moments help us feel loved, as well as loving.

Think about the following scenarios:

◆ *Last night Liz, who was watching television, went to bed much later than Gary, who wasn't feeling well. When Liz reached the bedroom, she absentmindedly put on the overhead light, plunked her book down on the bedside table, adjusted all the windows, ran water in the master bathroom instead of using the one down the hall, messed up when setting the alarm clock—accidentally releasing fifteen seconds of the sound of K-Rock Round the Clock, and generally made so much noise that Gary woke up and had a hard time falling back asleep. "Why does she have to be so selfish?" Gary thinks.*

◆ *Brandon, who is an early riser, lives with Gwen, who needs eight solid hours of sleep to feel fully rested. Before he goes to bed at night, Brandon leaves clothing for the morning hanging in the bathroom so he doesn't have to disturb his partner again and again by opening doors and drawers. When Gwen woke up this morning, one of the first things she noticed was the empty hanger hanging on the bathroom door. Remembering Brandon's obvious efforts not to wake her made Gwen smile and think, "He's so incredibly thoughtful."*

A good relationship is about good moments. Too many men and women have a "grand gesture" approach to love. They worry, sometimes obsessively, about the larger relationship moments: Valentine's Day, Christmas, birthdays, special dinners, really big fights. That's when they pay attention to what's taking place; that's when they declare their love. All of the in-between time, however, is not considered vital or important. Often, it's not considered at all.

Here is another relationship fact: *Most of the real work in relationships is taking place in quieter moments in smaller spaces.* Defrosting a can of orange juice for your partner because you noticed the pitcher in the refrigerator was almost empty. Keeping the phone line open when you know your partner is expecting a call. Helping your partner make the bed. Taking turns putting out food for the cat. Picking up your partner's laundry. These are classic examples of the absolutely smallest kind of stuff that can have a disproportionately large effect on the day-to-day experience of love in a partnership. Why? Because *every one of these smallest moments tells your partner, "I care about you."*

SMALL EVENTS SEND BIG MESSAGES

The "small stuff" of relationships—the small events and moments that make up each day—are the essence of a loving partnership. "Big stuff" such as love and attraction and integrity and commitment provide the framework—the necessary framework. But it is in the "small stuff" where our connections are given life and meaning.

Emmett and Janice are walking down the street. She stops to look in a store window. He stops also to put his arm around her and notice what she's noticing. Without uttering a single word, Emmett is clearly saying, "What's important to you is important to me: I want to share what you're thinking; I want to be in your world." This thirty seconds becomes a relationship event that is rich with meaningful messages.

Compare Emmett and Janice to Marc and Marnie, who are sitting poolside on their vacation in Mexico. Marnie is on her computer; Marc is on his cell phone. Marnie says, "I'm hungry. When are we going to eat?" Marc groans. This thirty seconds, including the groan, is another relationship event. And while there may be many messages embedded in this event, too, the one that seems most clear is: "we are not very connected to each other right now."

There is a message in these two scenarios for *you* also: *Nothing is unimportant.*

No one has needed to rent an airplane and write their messages in huge letters in the sky here, yet a multitude of important relationship messages are burning up the wires in these two "small" events. That's the thing about small events—they are always carrying a thousand times their weight in relationship messages.

BEING IN A RELATIONSHIP MEANS LIVING WITH ROUND-THE-CLOCK "RELATIONSHIP SURVEILLANCE"

You don't have to look for relationship messages with a microscope, and you don't have to crack them like some secret code. Whether you realize it or not, recognize it or not, believe it or not, your mind, your guts, and your heart are carefully and automatically monitoring and interpreting these messages like a supercomputer. And the impact of these messages is constantly reshaping your experience of partnership.

I call this process *"relationship surveillance."* This surveillance is not always fully conscious—there are times that it is completely *uncon-scious*—but it is always taking place. Your supercomputer never takes a day off. It never takes an hour off. It doesn't even take an occasional five-minute break. Even when you are fast asleep, your supercomputer is still collecting relationship messages: Is my partner touching me or not touching me? Is my partner relaxed or tense? Does my partner seem to be mad at me tonight? Is my partner grabbing the sheets and blankets selfishly? Is my partner making an excessive amount of noise? And so on. It is a round-the-clock, microscopic surveillance that is part of your complex human design. And that is why nothing is unimportant. You have to take the small stuff seriously.

MOVING CLOSER OR MOVING APART

The moments you have just witnessed between Emmett and Janice and Marc and Marnie are two small events. And neither one, in and of itself, is likely to make or break a relationship. Yet they still have relationship "weight"—an emotional weight that every partner feels. Look again at Marc and Marnie's event. Maybe Marc is tired from all the phone calls he's had to make, and will interact very differently once he's had an hour or two of rest. Maybe Marnie has a lot of stress right now from her job and her anxiety is making her unusually restless. We don't know. What we *do* know is that this particular relationship event, though it lasted no more than thirty seconds, gave Marc and Marnie an experience of *separateness*. Contrast this with the experience of Emmett and Janice. In their thirty-second event, they both had an experience of *connection*.

As these two simple scenarios illustrate, *EVERY small relationship event has two possible outcomes:*

> *1) It can reinforce a feeling of separateness, or . . .*
> *2) It can reinforce a feeling of connection.*

This is what I mean when I say that the event has emotional weight. A little bit closer, or a little more distant. A little bit more loving, or a little bit less loving. A little bit happier, a little bit less happy. A little bit more angry, a little bit less angry. A little bit more satisfied, a little bit less satisfied. A little bit more partnered, or a little bit less partnered. These small events keep our relationships in constant motion. And while that motion may be quite subtle, it is real, and it has consequences for the partnership.

THE BIG STUFF IS ONLY A BEGINNING

In the beginning of a new relationship, everything is pretty BIG. We think big, feel big, act big. LOVE, ROMANCE, SEX, COMMITMENT, THE FUTURE—these are where our energies are going, and this is completely appropriate. Beginnings are all about putting these important and necessary big pieces together. That's why we call them beginnings.

But what happens next? For some couples, there is no "next," not even if they are together for many months, or even years. Rafael and Tiffany—a couple I met last year at a relationship seminar of mine in Los Angeles—are one such couple. Rafael and Tiffany have been dating for three years, but they still have a "grand gesture" approach to their relationship. Their sense of connection comes from *big* things like sex, travel, expensive presents, and wildly romantic dinners. This is how they communicate, and this is how they resolve arguments. This is how they define their relationship, and this is how they try to maintain their relationship. I call this "living LARGE."

In just the past six months, Rafael and Tiffany have been to Aspen twice, to Tuscany, and to two regional film festivals. This probably sounds very exciting, romantic, and intense, yet the reality is that both Rafael and Tiffany are constantly struggling to stay in the relationship. Even though the attraction is very powerful, they are forever questioning whether or not this is, or should be, "the one." This confusion is what brought them to my seminar.

What is completely missing from this picture, keeping this couple in a constant state of uncertainty and high drama, is a small-stuff approach to relationship maintenance. Rafael and Tiffany rally around the big stuff, and they do a great job of it. When they make a big connection they feel swept up in powerful tides of love, and it is not unusual to hear one of them exclaim, "I feel like I've fallen in love all over again!" But when those tides subside, they are still left feeling empty and depleted. That's because the small stuff—the stuff that slowly accumulates over time into a solid relationship core—is regularly ignored. Simply put, they haven't learned to take care of each other in smaller ways.

Don't get me wrong. You need the big stuff to get you started in a relationship. But it's the small stuff that gives your relationship its legs.

RELATIONSHIP MAINTENANCE AND "CAPILLARY ACTION"

Relationship maintenance. What does this phrase mean to you? When you start to understand that every single relationship event—even the smallest gesture—has some emotional weight, your approach to relationship maintenance begins to change.

Men and women who ascribe to the "grand gesture" approach are always trying to reach their partners' hearts by going through the large blood vessels. But truly loving couples know that love—the kind that holds firm, and grows over time—flows from one partner to the other every single day at the capillary level. Grand gestures certainly have their place; however, it is the steady stream of smaller signals, forming rich networks of attention and consideration, that makes a partner feel truly valued.

Capillary action gives a relationship its life and health. It's not about the size of your heart or the power of your attraction, it's about *flow*. Love has to flow steadily through the capillaries so your partner can feel your love in a *consistent* way. The big stuff doesn't create that sense of consistency. It can "wow" you for a while, but it doesn't build *trust*, and it doesn't keep the connection feeling vital. That only happens when there is a stream of consistent loving messages that are being communicated in smaller moments through smaller, daily events.

Relationship maintenance is a small-stuff process.

RELATIONSHIP TERMITES

Every small moment that is shared by two people is a relationship opportunity. It is a chance to fortify the connection—to make a richer, stronger bond. Every small moment that is missed is a *lost* opportunity. And every small moment that is mishandled or ignored can create what I call a *"relationship termite."*

My wife and I know all about termites. When we rented our first apartment together, we noticed a few insects by the front window sill. We didn't know what they were. Within a few months, the window frame had been cored. Tiny little things taking tiny little bites out of a huge, strong structure. But there is nothing tiny about the effects over time.

When I think back now about our experience in that apartment, I realize that I needed to see those termites with my own eyes and witness their destructive potential to learn a larger lesson about termite power in loving relationships. Being single taught me a lot of lessons about relationships, but it didn't teach me about relationship termites. Those little bugs in the window gave me an image I could relate to.

Loving partners check regularly for "relationship termites," because that's what the relationship process is about. Too many relationships are weakened by termites. These couples aren't fighting about money or sex; they are honestly engaged in daily conflicts of the "Why can't you put the top back on the toothpaste?" variety.

Think about this the next time you are living through a small relationship moment and telling yourself, *"It doesn't matter."* "It doesn't matter if I don't ask his/her opinion first." "It doesn't matter if I'm paying close attention or not." "It doesn't matter if I'm 100 percent honest right now." "It doesn't matter if I forget to call to say I'm running late." "It doesn't matter if I don't pick up my dirty socks." "It doesn't matter if I don't say 'I love you' this very moment." "It doesn't matter if I let the litter box go one more day." "It doesn't matter if I don't return his/her phone call this very instant." "It doesn't matter if I don't stop what I'm doing right now to listen more carefully to what he/she is saying." "It doesn't matter if I don't replace the roll of toilet paper." "It doesn't matter if I eat that piece of cake she/he was saving." "It doesn't matter if I dodge the grocery shopping." "It doesn't matter if I pour myself a drink and don't offer to pour her/him one." "It doesn't matter if I'm a little late getting home most nights." "It doesn't matter if I don't make the bed today." "It doesn't matter if I don't send his/her sister a thank-you note." "It doesn't matter if I wake her/him up in the middle of the night." "It doesn't matter if I track a little bit of mud through the house on a rainy day." "It doesn't matter if I don't always say thank you." "It doesn't matter if I hog the hot water this morning." "It doesn't matter if I hog the blankets tonight." "It doesn't matter if I let the dirty dishes pile up in the sink today." "It doesn't matter if I don't take out the recycling this week." "It doesn't matter if I don't fill the ice cube trays every time I empty them." "It doesn't matter if I leave the lights on when I'm not using them."

When I look at this list, I see a giant mound of termites. Can you see this, too?

Rationalizing the Termites

Here's another kind of termite mound, the mound that builds when we dismiss our own small needs and concerns and tell ourselves, *"I don't really mind . . ."* "I don't really mind that my partner doesn't always listen." "I don't really mind that my partner doesn't always say thank you." "I don't really mind that my partner makes plans without asking me first." "I don't really mind that my partner doesn't call when he/she is running late." "I don't really mind that I'm always the one who buys stamps." "I don't really mind that I'm always the one who washes the dishes." "I don't really mind that my partner doesn't leave me enough hot water for my shower." "I don't really mind that my partner plays loud music when I'm trying to work." "I don't really mind that my partner runs up the phone bill." "I don't really mind that I'm always the one paying for the expensive stuff." "I don't really mind that my partner doesn't always introduce me to his/her friends at parties." "I don't really mind that I'm always the second one to use the sink." "I don't really mind that my partner fills the house with magazines no one reads." "I don't really mind that my partner keeps fiddling with my computer software." "I don't really mind that my partner doesn't regularly ask for my opinion." "I don't really mind that I'm the one who has to make most of the little decisions." "I don't really mind that my partner sometimes cuts me off mid-sentence." "I don't really mind that I'm always cleaning little hairs out of the sink." "I don't really mind that I'm always the one who turns out all the lights." "I don't really mind that my partner just ate the last chocolate chip cookie."

These are the kinds of termites we are particularly good at rationalizing to protect our partner and protect our feeling of being connected. We tell ourselves things like, "She's doing the best she can." "He didn't learn this as a kid." "She has parents who set a bad example." "He has sibling issues." "He doesn't realize how much hot water he's using." "She doesn't realize I was waiting to share that chocolate chip cookie." "He hates to cook, and I really don't mind." "She doesn't realize that she hasn't introduced me to these friends." "He loses track of time when he's on the phone." "She probably couldn't find a phone to call me and tell me she'd be home late." "He's under a lot of pressure and the loud music helps him relax." "She's more stressed about money than I am." Do any of these rationalizations sound familiar? There's just one problem, and it is not a small one: Rationalizations can make you feel better, but they don't make your *relationship* better. *Rationalizing termites doesn't eliminate the termites, it just drives them underground where they can chew closer to the relationship foundation.*

De-Bugging Your Relationship, One Termite at a Time

Living in southern California, I have learned something else about termites: Every house has them. Every *relationship* also has its termites. Emotional connections are always vulnerable in that way. So I don't expect you (or me, for that matter) to build a relationship that is termite-free. It isn't possible. What I *do* expect, however, is that you take the termite problem seriously, and do your best to minimize the damage by adopting a small-stuff approach to relationship maintenance.

You might want to take a few moments right now to get a pen and paper and make a list of the termites that have been feasting on your relationship lately. Think about the little things you tend to dismiss, ignore, or rationalize away. Think about the little things that upset you, annoy you, confuse you, or make you uncomfortable—even the very smallest things. Having this list, and keeping it current, keeps your termites in plain sight where they can't do as much damage. This is not always fun, but it keeps you in touch with your little struggles and gives you more opportunity to squash a few bugs.

YOU AND YOUR PARTNER DON'T HAVE THE SAME SMALL STUFF

Many of us have a difficult time taking our partner's small stuff seriously. It's hard sometimes to fully understand someone else's reality, even when we *want* to understand it. Yet the trick in relationships is to find out which small stuff is most important to each partner and to make room for that stuff. This is part of what *not* being single is all about.

Consider, as one example, your partner's anxieties. Your partner's anxieties represent the kind of small stuff that creates ongoing issues in relationships. My wife, for example, is very sensitive to the amount of floodlight that surrounds our house at night. She feels safer knowing that the place is well lit. This is not something that I would pay very much attention to, and before I met my wife weeks could go by before I would get around to changing a bulb. Yet I know now that my wife has enough anxiety around this issue that if I neglect to change a bulb, she can interpret it as though I am neglecting her or not interested in protecting her and helping her feel safe. So I have learned to pay more attention, and to make sure that burnt-out bulbs are immediately replaced.

My wife is not the only one in our relationship who has small-stuff anxieties. I have a long list of my own—equally important to me. We all have this kind of anxiety about *something*. How these anxieties are handled is an ongoing part of the relationship process.

Paying Attention to Your Partner's Anxieties, and Other Big Small Stuff

Your partner's anxieties are an important example of "big small stuff." Big small stuff may not have the heft of relationship "heavyweights" such as love, sex, values, goals, money, or spirituality, but they are still dangerous to ignore.

How do you handle your partner's anxieties? Do you take them seriously, and try to accommodate them wherever possible? Or do you dismiss them easily because they're not *your* anxieties. And what about *your* anxieties? Do you try to hide them from your partner, or do you treat them as a part of you that your partner needs to accept and learn to live with?

Fact: You don't have to understand your partner's anxieties, and your partner doesn't have to understand yours. *Fact:* You don't have to embrace your partner's anxieties, and your partner doesn't have to embrace yours. *Fact:* Maybe, from where you sit, some of these anxieties are slightly irrational, illogical, or overblown. But these anxieties are real, and they need to be acknowledged and accommodated. Otherwise, this is the kind of material that can create a powerful sense of separateness, driving a wedge between two people, even if they love each other. Other examples of "big small stuff" include sleep issues, household chores, schedules, environmental preferences (lighting, windows, thermostat, etc.), and personal "stuff." These are all relationship hot buttons that have the power to seriously tip the scales of partnership in both a positive *and* a negative direction, depending on how they are handled.

Household Stuff ("The Bed Is a Mess!")

Bernard and Jesse are a typical working couple. They both have very demanding jobs that leave them fairly exhausted much of the time. But, like most couples, they still need to find time for the basics like food shopping, housecleaning, laundry, and cooking. Here's one of their problems: Bernard refuses to help Jesse make the bed. Bernard grew up in a household where he was not allowed to go out and play with his friends until he had cleaned his room and made his bed, and his efforts often failed parental inspections. Twenty years later, he still has a lot of residual anger about the "laws" of his childhood household. Being defiant about making the bed today is his way of dealing with his unprocessed anger. But Jesse is now the one who is really angry. She resents having a messy looking bedroom, and she resents the fact that she usually caves in and makes the bed herself. She gets particularly angry when Bernard says things like, "What's the point of making the bed? It's just going to get messed up again in a few hours."

Household chores have to get done. And if they are not done in a fair and balanced way, they can land your partnership in the relationship hospital. Are you quietly handling more than your share of the household chores while collecting a heaping pile of resentment? It's time to ask for more help. Are you taking advantage of your partner's good nature when it comes to chores? It's time to balance the load. Are you enacting a stereotypical division of labor that's putting most of the burden on just one partner? (We'll talk about this more when we get to *Secret #4*.) Come out of the dark ages, roll up your sleeves, and start dealing with household stuff. Stop making excuses, being irresponsible, and falling into lopsided, unfair arrangements that only reinforce feelings of separateness.

Environment Stuff ("It's Hot in Here!")

Carla and Bryan moved in together one year ago, and ever since then they have been playing "the thermostat game." Here's how the game is played: When Carla comes home from her office every day, the first thing she does is set the thermostat the way she likes it. When Bryan arrives home thirty or forty minutes later, he eyes the thermostat and waits till Carla is in a different room before turning it down just a few degrees. Then he hopes she won't notice. If Carla does notice, she covertly readjusts it. Back and forth it goes, with no admission of subterfuge ever taking place. Last night Bryan actually waited until Carla was asleep before turning the thermostat down one last time. When Carla woke up in the middle of the night, the room was freezing and her throat was sore.

It can be very hard for two individuals, with very different needs and preferences, to come to terms with the daily issues that surface around the household environment:

- Do the windows stay opened or closed?
- Do the shades stay up or down?
- Which lights stay on and which stay off?
- What goes where in the cabinets, drawers, and refrigerator?
- Do we use the air conditioner? Or the fans?
- How full can the closets get?
- At what temperature do we set the thermostat?

And the list goes on. Think about everything that is coming into play here: sensitivity, habits, health requirements, emotional issues, anxieties, philosophies, financial concerns, *control, control, control.* Get the picture? The *big* picture? This is big small stuff. How do you handle these issues in your relationship? Here are some suggestions:

- Understand that probably neither of you are right; you are just different.
- Find friendly ways to negotiate and compromise.
- Don't expect your partner to read your mind.
- Don't always insist on your way, and be willing to compromise on those things that don't really mean that much to you.
- Try to keep your priorities in order.
- Be prepared to wear a sweater, take off your jacket, or adjust your sleeping arrangement.

Social Stuff ("But We Went Out Last Night!")

Alexandra has a problem that has been growing slowly but steadily ever since she started living with Philip: Philip doesn't always consult her before he makes plans. He invites friends over for dinner because he loves to cook for lots of people. He accepts invitations to parties because he loves to socialize with Alexandra. He buys tickets to concerts because he and Alexandra adore live music performances. But he always tells Alexandra after the plans have been made. Sometimes this works for Alexandra, but more often it doesn't, and she gets angry that Philip hasn't asked her about her scheduling needs. Then, of course, she starts feeling guilty. Philip thinks he is doing what Alexandra would want, but he never stops and takes the time to make sure. When it comes to scheduling, he is still acting like a single person. Small stuff, big problem.

It's easy to plan your day when you are single. You work when you have to work, then you fill in the rest of the day as it suits you. But when you are part of a couple, and the details of your partner's Day Runner become as important as the details of your Day-at-a-Glance, schedules are bound to collide. Who stays home to let the plumber in? Who races home to walk the dog? Do we go out tonight, or do we stay home? Do we see your friends, my friends, or *our* friends? How much time do we spend with family? How much time do we spend apart?

To create an effective partnership, you have to deal with *three* different schedules: your schedule, your partner's schedule, and your joint schedule as a couple—the ways you will meet in the middle. All three schedules have equal weight, and problems start when any one of them is ignored or given short shrift. This is, admittedly, a balancing act that requires ongoing awareness and consideration. Yet the simple act of *acknowledging* that there are always *three* schedules to be considered in every decision is a huge first step to handling the potential conflicts.

Sleep Stuff ("I Hate This Mattress!")

Sleep. We all need it, and most of us don't get enough of it. But your specific needs, and how you meet those needs, are likely to be very different than your partner's needs and how your partner meets those needs. Maybe you need six hours to function effectively and your partner needs eight. Maybe you need a super-firm mattress and your partner prefers a featherbed. Maybe your partner could sleep through an earthquake while you are roused by every noise. Maybe you like to fall asleep watching television while your partner needs the room to be completely dark. Maybe your partner likes to go to bed early and wake up early while you are a night owl who can sleep till noon the next day. While it may seem rather small, it is the kind of small stuff that creates large conflict.

Sleep happens to be my biggest small stuff issue, and I've written about this before. When it comes to sleep, I have the worst combination of needs: I feel horrible if I don't get at least eight hours of sleep, and every sound in the universe can wake me up. I am always appreciative of my wife's sensitivity to my hypersensitivity, as well as her willingness to address the smallest sleep issues such as open windows, white noise machines, gentler alarm clocks, special pillows.

Do you take your partner's sleep stuff seriously? Are you constantly exploring ways to make sure that each of you is getting what he or she needs? Or is sleep stuff a "big small problem" in your relationship? Are you often angry, for example, because your sleep routines are out of synch? Do you accuse your partner of being lazy if he/she needs more hours than you need? Do you neglect your partner's complaints about your mattress because it works just fine for you? And what about your own sleep requirements? Do you respect them and take them seriously, or are you giving up too much of what you need to stay in good health and function effectively? There is such a thing as too much compromise, particularly when it comes to sleep.

Personal Stuff ("What Did You Do With My Stuff?")

Gardena is thoroughly frustrated because she can't find her favorite slippers. William is ticked off because the newspaper he was reading somehow ended up in the trash. Ellen could scream because her favorite crystal vase has been moved from the shelf where she put it last week. Carlos is ready to chew out his girlfriend because she just rearranged his collection of family photographs. Four different examples of a classic relationship drama.

None of us enters into a relationship completely unencumbered by small stuff. We have small neurotic stuff and small family stuff and small work stuff and small quirky personality stuff and small sex stuff and small sleep stuff and small food stuff and on and on and on. But we also have just plain *stuff*. Teddy bears and cappucino machines and books and clothes and tennis racquets and hair clips and notepads and gumball dispensers and trinkets from old summer vacations. You know what I'm talking about.

How do you deal with your partner's personal stuff? Do you have a respectful, hands-off-until-given-permission-to-do-otherwise approach, or do you view most of it as a collection of "unimportants," "rearrangeables," and "disposables"? Sometimes the way we handle the very smallest personal stuff can be a powerful symbol of our acceptance (or lack of acceptance), our boundaries (or lack of boundaries), our respect (or lack of respect), our care (or lack of care), and our desire to be a true partner (or lack of desire). Don't get tripped up by the tiniest stuff. Even a plastic tchotchke that only cost $1.79 can, in the eyes of your partner, be very big small stuff.

The Old, Single Stuff ("Do We Have To Order Pizza Again?")

If you have been "living single" for a long time (be that with, or without a partner), you have probably built up a long inventory of small-stuff preferences. You have your favorite blend of coffee, your favorite Chinese restaurant, your favorite Thursday night sitcom, and so on. And, in their own small ways, most of these things are important to you.

In the "thrills" of a new relationship, when real love—the thing we crave most—is entering into your life, some of these preferences suddenly seem trivial or meaningless. And many get put on the back burner. But as time passes, and our heart grows content, we start thinking about those small-stuff preferences again.

This shift is not a *bad* thing. It does not mean that the magic is gone, or that you have fallen out of love. To the contrary, this shift is a good and healthy sign—a sign telling you that your relationship is on solid ground, and that you are trusting in your heart of hearts that the "big stuff" is in place. This shift doesn't happen *until* the big stuff is in place. Yet the shift does create conflict, and this conflict needs to be taken seriously.

What do you do about your smaller stuff preferences now that you feel the shift? Does being in a partnership mean being a little bit angry all of the time because you had to give up all of the small-stuff preferences that you hold dear? Does it mean never again having a slice of your favorite Numero Uno deep dish pizza because your partner prefers thin crust pizza from Domino's? No. It just means that you have more small stuff on the table to negotiate in a fair and balanced way. This week you go to Lucky Dragon and fill your plate (yum!); next week you go to Imperial Palace and eat like a good sport (yuck!).

You tape your favorite sitcom and watch it a little bit later; next week, you switch. You make two different pots of coffee and keep one warm in a thermos while the other is brewing. You figure it out. *What you DON'T do is belittle your partner's preferences because they are different than yours, or abandon your small-stuff preferences just because they are small.*

WORKING THE SMALL STUFF: A SIMPLE GUIDE

So how do you work all of this small stuff? How do you stay on track day after day, month after month, year after year? It isn't as complicated as it seems. The key, not surprisingly, is *micromanagement.* These guidelines should help . . .

1. Pay Attention

When the big stuff is in place, it is easy to rest on your laurels and think that everything is going to be just fine. But now you know that small stuff is serious stuff—serious enough to topple the big stuff over time. So start paying attention. Pay attention to your partner's preferences, concerns, and anxieties, however small they may seem. Tune in to your partner's habits and schedule. Think about constantly balancing the workload. Pay attention to common areas where small conflicts might arise, such as the kitchen, the closets, the telephones, and the thermostat. Become an "expert" in the small stuff of your relationship.

2. Respect Your Partner's Reality

No two people have the same small stuff, but that doesn't make it any less important. Being a better partner means learning to *accept* and *prioritize* little issues that have real weight for your partner. Don't diminish, discredit, or disregard your partner's small stuff just because it isn't yours. Don't be an emotional bully who says, "Don't bother me unless it's something big." These "solutions" are not resolutions, and they quickly lead to bigger problem stuff.

3. Process Immediately

The key to working with the small stuff is *active processing*—taking immediate action as each piece of stuff surfaces. There is no "good time" to deal with uncomfortable stuff, even when it is small. So work in the moment and minimize the long-term impact of relationship termites.

4. Keep One Eye on YOUR Stuff

Don't discount or neglect your own small stuff. You have to voice your smallest discomforts and your tiniest concerns; never stop asking ask for little things if they are important to you. Otherwise, you create a large pile of discontent that keeps you feeling separate from your partner.

5. Look for LITTLE Solutions

Small-stuff problems need small-stuff solutions: an acknowledgment, a gesture, a brief conversation, a simple compromise, an apology. Don't turn every tiny issue into a larger-than-life drama. As long as it hasn't been accumulating, small stuff shouldn't be overwhelming.

6. Appreciate Small Loving Moments

A lot of the small stuff is *good* stuff. Take time to "smell the small stuff"—time to acknowledge and enjoy the little loving moments that are a part of your relationship. Fully digest these little relationship moments. These are the things that are too easy to take for granted in a good relationship. Reinforce the positive.

7. Create More Small Loving Moments

Don't wait for the big moments to do loving things. Every small, loving gesture is a little dab of relationship superglue that fortifies your attachment and your sense of partnership. It takes very little effort to create small loving moments, and the payoff is disproportionately large.

8. Don't Give Up on the Small Stuff

The small-stuff process is an endless one. At times it can be frustrating, and at times it can seem exhausting. But it is far more exhausting, as you may very well know, to be forever trying to bring your relationship back from the brink because you've let the small stuff slide. Working the small stuff gives your love depth, strength, and character. It is a huge chunk of the partnership experience. So make a commitment to giving the small stuff—the good stuff *and* the tough stuff—the attention it deserves.

SECRET #2:

Take Off The Masks

. ◆ .

Partnership doesn't work if you can't reveal your true self to your partner.
And I am stating this right up front because I know how scary this sentence is for so many people. I promise you that it only gets easier after this.

A truly loving and *effective* partnership requires an honest connection—one that can grow and deepen over time. And such a connection is not possible if we are living behind masks, no matter how carefully we have constructed them. I know this must make sense to you.
Yet I also know that so many of us cling tenaciously to those masks,
even as we try so hard to build a partnership that will last.

Let me begin with my own confession: I have always had a very difficult time letting another person see who I am. And the older I got, the
more difficult it was for me to risk visibility. In fact, until I met my wife,
I would have to say that I *always* played it safe. Sometimes I was playing the part of the good friend, sometimes I was playing the part of the
relationship expert, sometimes I was playing the part of the well-
intentioned boyfriend. Sometimes I was playing the part of the "sensitive" male, and sometimes I was playing the part of the difficult male.
But I was always playing a part, and never being myself. At times I

played those parts so well that I started to lose sight of who I really was.

I'm not very proud of the fact that I lived so much of my life hiding behind various masks, but what makes it a little easier for me to admit this to you here is knowing that my experience is not all that unusual. *MOST of us keep things hidden, even from our partners.* Sometimes it's our past that we are concealing; sometimes it's our hopes for the future. And sometimes it's important feelings and emotions. Some of us are hiding our failures, and some of us are hiding our fears. Some of us are hiding the grey roots in our hair or our cellulite. Some of us are hiding an addiction. Some of us are hiding our passion for chocolate. Some of us are hiding our sentimental natures. Some of us are hiding a collection of kinky movies. Some of us are hiding our debts. And some of us are hiding our money.

How much intimacy are you prepared to risk? How much of yourself—little pieces and big pieces—do you reveal to your partner, and how much do you keep hidden? Stop for a moment, and think seriously about these questions. Most people foolishly believe that they can choose what they will or will not share with their partners, and that these choices don't have an impact on the relationship. But that's not how intimacy works.

MASKS GET IN THE WAY OF DEEPER CONNECTIONS

Relationships are never static; they are either moving in the direction of deeper connection and intimacy or moving in the direction of separateness and disconnection. *The feelings and facts we choose to withhold from our partners fuel the engine of disconnection; the feelings and facts we are willing to share bring us closer.* This is basic relationship math. And this is why it is so crucial that we learn to take off the masks. In many ways, you don't really have a choice—not if you want to build a partnership you can trust.

Take Off the Masks

Those of us who have managed to peel off some of our masks with our partners know the special feeling of coming home to a place where we are fully welcome. When we step out into the world every day, whether it's going to work or going to the supermarket, our defenses are raised because we believe it is unsafe or unwise to be too trusting. But when we come home to our partners, those defenses need to melt and make space for our hearts to connect. If those defenses *don't* melt—if we remain guarded in our most potentially intimate settings—we are consistently cheating both ourselves and our partners of an opportunity for more heartfelt connection. We are not reaching out, and we are not letting our partner in. And that leads to real isolation.

Every Mask Has an Emotional Cost

This doesn't mean that you are not entitled to have your secrets. Some things are not meant to be shared, and some things are not ready to be shared. What it does mean is that every secret has a hidden cost—an emotional cost that is deducted directly from your experience of partnership. As secrets—large and small—collect over time, the feeling of separation intensifies. Too many secrets, and they start to act like walls. *You can't keep hiding pieces of yourself and expect that it won't have an impact.*

It took me a very long time to understand this. For many years of my life, I thought I could wear my various masks as I saw fit without affecting the outcome of my relationships. I believed that special chemistry, good sex, and romantic love were the driving forces in those relationships. When I started to feel more and more isolated and lonely within the relationship, I either blamed my partners, or chalked it up to the paradox of human nature. And when those relationships disintegrated, as they *all* did, it never occurred to me that my masks were responsible for part of that process. I didn't understand that masks deprive connections of their depth and richness. I

41

didn't understand the cost of letting fear and shame hide a more genuine, lovable self. I didn't understand that scripts help us avoid real intimacy. It was so much easier to point a finger at the peculiar and ephemeral nature of love.

HOW INTIMATE DO YOU WANT TO GET?

Everyone, of course, has different ideas about how intimate they can be. Cynthia, for example, insists on sharing a bathroom with her husband Carl even though there are enough bathrooms in the house for each to have their own. Ever since her unsuccessful first marriage, Cynthia has been aware of the relationship risks that two people take when they start hiding even small insignificant pieces of their lives—like brushing and flossing. This approach works for Cynthia and Carl. This is not about kinky stuff—when nature calls, each enjoys their privacy. But they don't hide their imperfections from each other, and they don't hide their humanness. Cynthia doesn't want Carl to have to hide the hairs that are disappearing from his scalp and collecting on his brush. And she doesn't want to have to hide her morning naked face. This may sound very simple, or even silly, but it is definitely part of what makes their bond strong.

Elaina is very unlike Cynthia in her approach. She doesn't want her husband to see her plucking her eyebrows, flossing her teeth, or applying astringent. As far as she's concerned nobody needs to see her tweezers, her Epilady, her Retin-A cream, or her Proxi-brush. In front of her husband, she never wants to look like a "work in progress." If she can help it, she wants him to always see her at her very best.

The point, of course, is whether or not we let our small secrets take over and control our relationships. Intimacy is about intimacy. It's about allowing your partner to see your imperfections; it's about allowing your partner to see you without a mask. When we get into the most trouble is when our masks become so all-encompassing that our part-ners can't possibly see who we really are and what we really feel.

This doesn't mean that tonight, when you get home from work, you need to redesign your house and merge your bathrooms. That bath-room may be the only few square feet in your home that is yours and yours alone, and you deserve to protect and maintain that. It just means you need to start acknowledging what you hide, why you choose to keep certain areas hidden, and the impact those choices are having on your relationship.

In which of the following areas are you less than open with your partner?

- Your feelings
- Your ideas
- Your needs
- Your hopes and dreams
- Your finances
- Your friends and family
- Your creativity
- Your passions
- Your personal truth

- Your fears
- Your opinions
- Your history
- Your sexuality
- Your body
- Your work
- Your tastes
- Your spirituality

Think about why and how each of these issues affects your relationship.

Masks Make Us Intimate Strangers with a Fragile Bond

I have been writing books about relationships for almost twenty years, and I have interviewed countless couples during those years. I have also spent a great deal of time with couples who are friends, neighbors, professional acquaintances, and relatives. One of the most difficult things about this is when I am in the presence of two people who are "together" as a couple, yet painfully separate. They may be sleeping together, living together, or married forever, yet they have remained strangers to each other in so many ways, keeping huge chunks of themselves hidden from each other. Intimate strangers, still hiding behind their masks.

It is painful and scary for me to spend time with couples like this; I can only imagine how difficult it must be for them. What I have learned from spending time with these couples is that holding up the masks keeps any relationship fragile. The future always feels terribly uncertain.

It's hard to "be ourselves" in the very beginning of a relationship, and often, it isn't a priority. Dating rituals typically take precedence. We feel protected by those rituals, and it's easier to stay in our assigned roles. But sooner or later we have to let our hair down and start being real. Otherwise we find ourselves trapped in permanently stilted roles of our own creation.

Intimate Sharing vs. Inappropriate "Dumping"

When a relationship is just beginning, masks are appropriate and self-protective. You don't want to show up on a first date carrying a laundry list of personal flaws, shortcomings, and deep dark secrets. And you don't want to put all of this on the table by the end of week number one. I have to acknowledge that I know a lot of people who do just that. They can't wait to tell a prospective partner about every person they have ever had sex with, or every childhood trauma they have endured, or every medication they have ever put into their bloodstream, or every enemy they have ever made, etc. There is something both painful and scary about this "full disclosure," too.

People who rush to disclose the most intimate details of their life claim their behavior is self-protective. "If you can't handle every bit of this, I might as well know right now," is the explanation. But I call this "inappropriate sharing." You might call it "dumping." And I see this as a self-sabotaging mechanism—a way to frighten off any prospective partner and *guarantee* that a relationship will never get off the ground.

I could never endorse this kind of extreme behavior. Yet I also know that moving forward in a relationship—out of your single and separate state and into a more gratifying partnered state—is a necessary process of challenging your own masks and taking them down piece by piece.

WHERE DO YOU DO YOUR BEST HIDING?

Stop for a moment right now and think about the various "hiding places" you have come to rely on.

- Do you hide behind your job or your hectic lifestyle?
- Do you hide behind tailored business suits, or layers and layers of stylized clothing and accessories?
- Do you hide behind newspapers, books, and magazines?
- Do you hide behind your endless hobbies?
- Do you hide behind your professional persona?
- Do you hide behind your bravado or your well-practiced rap?
- Do you hide behind your constant joking?
- Do you hide behind sex?
- Do you hide behind food? Behind alcohol? Behind drugs?
- Do you hide behind your words?
- Do you hide behind your money?
- Do you hide behind your computer?
- Do you hide behind your friends? Behind your siblings? Behind your mother? Behind your kids?

If you are going to slowly come out of hiding, it really helps to know where you do your best hiding. Shining a flashlight into those various nooks and crannies can be eye-opening, liberating, and very healing. And it widens the access road to partnership.

SOMETIMES MASKS ARE HIDING OUR GREATEST ASSETS

Here is a concept that is hard for people to grasp: *Often we are hiding the most endearing and lovable parts of ourselves.* For example:

- We're not afraid to show our anger, but we're afraid to show our vulnerability, or . . .
- We're not afraid to show our tough side, but we're afraid to show our tenderness, or . . .
- We're not afraid to show our biceps, but we're afraid to show our soft underbellies, or . . .
- We're not afraid to show our helplessness, but we're afraid to show our smarts.

When we do this, we present our partners with distorted pictures—lopsided caricatures of who we are. Consider the following scenarios:

◆ *Geoff is thinking about breaking up with Joyce because he finds her conversations boring. In truth, Joyce is a funny woman with many interesting opinions and ideas, but she only lets her hair down with her closest girlfriends. Why does Joyce hide all of this from Geoff? Because she thinks her opinions and ideas can be intimidating and not "lady-like." How different their relationship could be if Geoff had a chance to experience the true Joyce.*

◆ *Mark and Betsy have never been able to have an honest conversation about money. Mark doesn't want Betsy to know the truth about his credit card debt, but he also resents it when Betsy suggests having dinner at expensive restaurants. Why does Mark need to hide his financial reality? Because he believes that to be a good partner he should "have it all together" in the financial department. Yet what Mark is doing is depriving Betsy of the opportunity to be a true partner.*

46

◆ *Delores and Tom have been together for six years, and she still hasn't told him what to do to help her reach orgasm. Why does she keep this information from Tom? Because she thinks it is too much work for him, that it will make him feel pressured, and that it isn't "crucial" to her enjoyment of sex. But Delores is kidding herself, and her hidden resentment tends to creep out in other ways.*

◆ *Tiffany and Robert have been married for six months, and Tiffany still feels as though she is concealing the fact that she is the mother of a seven-year-old child, Blake, even though Blake lives with them. She tries to handle most of her "parenting" when Robert isn't home. She never discusses Blake's school issues or anything else with her new husband. When Robert is home she encourages Blake to spend more and more time watching television alone in his room. She's not sure why she is doing this; all she knows is that she is afraid that if Robert sees her as a mother, with the kind of human everyday problems that parents have, he will find her less desirable.*

We all have our reasons for hiding these parts of ourselves, but these parts are a big part of who we are. Think about how important it is to share, with your partner, pictures of friends and family, where you went to school, and the house you grew up in. Think about how important it is to share stories about meaningful people, places, and events from your past. It does something for your heart to make these connections with someone who loves you. Yet at the same time, we can hide other things about us that are so *huge*. And by keeping things in hiding, we deprive our partners of the opportunity to genuinely know, understand, accept, and care about us.

I can't promise you that your partner is going to adore, embrace, and celebrate every single bit of who you are. But if you are trying to create a bond that will hold up to years of relationship challenges, there is only one road that will get you there, and masks are not welcome on that road.

WHY IS IT SO HARD TO TAKE OFF THE MASKS?

There are a lot of different reasons why we have so much difficulty being more honest, more clear, more direct, and more true to who we are.

- Sometimes we hide parts of ourselves out of habit.
- Sometimes we hide parts of ourselves because we think we're *supposed to.*
- Sometimes we hide parts of ourselves because we think those parts are shameful.
- Sometimes we hide parts of ourselves because we think those parts are not welcome.
- Sometimes we hide parts of ourselves because we're afraid of being a burden.
- Sometimes we hide parts of ourselves because we're afraid to rock the boat.
- Sometimes we hide parts of ourselves because we're trying to be who (we think) our partner wants us to be.
- Sometimes we hide parts of ourselves because we think they are unattractive flaws.
- Sometimes we hide parts of ourselves because we're afraid of being different than our partner.

Masks We Wear Out of Habit and Bad Reflex

Alex would never consider talking to his new partner about his fear of failure and his discomfort at being in new situations. He has wrestled with this fear all of his adult life, and it's something he just accepts as part of who he is. Alex is used to having internal struggles. And being single most of his life, he is also used to handling these struggles alone. Having a partner hasn't changed his mindset.

Take Off the Masks

Men and women who have had a single-person mindset for a long time can get very used to keeping things to themselves. (And you don't have to be single to have a single-person mindset.) We learn to handle our own "stuff" and even when we find a loving partner, we don't consider turning to them for help, support, or advice in the areas we have learned to deal with by ourselves. We don't do this intentionally; it's just a bad reflex. What we never consider is the lost opportunity for making a closer connection.

Pause here and consider these two questions: What are some of your bad mask reflexes? How do these reflexes push your partner away?

Masks We're "Supposed" to Wear

Candace is afraid of showing a man how strong she is because she's been told that "Men are afraid of successful, independent women." When she's with her boyfriend, she often plays the part of the cute, helpless "girl." When men ask her questions, she often goes so far as to "dumb down" her answer. Later, she is always angry at herself for doing this—and angry at the men, too—but she also thinks she is doing the appropriate thing.

Consider all of the messages we have digested during our lifetimes that tell us what masks we're *supposed to* wear—messages from television, movies, magazines, friends, and family. "Never let 'em see you sweat." "Smart women intimidate men." "Playing dumb is sexy." "What you do with your money is *your* business." These messages powerfully affect our ability to take down our masks, creating barriers to more genuine connection.

Ask yourself: What "supposed to" messages are still controlling your behavior, encouraging you to wear different masks? Are these messages and your masks controlling your partner's behavior too?

Hiding Our Shameful Past—and Present

Byron has been in therapy for almost two years, and he knows this has made it possible for him to find a new, more loving relationship. Yet he has still not told his partner that he sees a therapist because he is so afraid of being harshly judged. Byron agonized for years before starting therapy, because in his family, "only crazy people go to therapists." Byron knows he is not "crazy," but he still lives in fear of the label. What he never considers is that his partner might appreciate his commitment to therapy. Or that sharing his positive experience and positive opinion of therapy with his partner might open doors for her.

Do you treat your life as though it is an open book, or do you have a closet full of secrets you could never imagine sharing with *anyone*, not even your loving partner? Emotional problems such as depression, compulsions, or chronic anxiety? A history of abuse? Addictions? Financial struggles? Problematic relatives? All of these things play an active role in your partnership, even if you think you are hiding all of the details where your partner can't find them.

Some of this material needs to be processed with a professional therapist before it can be shared with a partner, and some of it *shouldn't* be shared. But it is important to understand how the masks you build around this material help or hinder your partnership.

Take some time here to think about these two questions: What secrets from your past, and present, might be having an adverse affect on your ability to be a fully present, connected partner? How might these secrets be making your partner feel shut out from important parts of your life?

Hiding What Isn't Welcome

Shelley is so angry at her sister-in-law Bobbi that she sees red at the mere mention of her name. Bobbi uses Shelley's house as her personal playpen, eating all her snacks, drinking her favorite wines, making hours of phone calls, and screwing up the VCR. Yet Shelley's husband seems oblivious to almost everything Bobbi does, and this freezes Shelley in her tracks. How can she complain if her husband isn't having a problem, too? If she says anything she'll feel like she is too emotional, too selfish, or not family-oriented enough. She is worried that she will appear to be making a scene.

Once again, we're dealing with old messages here, messages that encourage us to build masks. "If you can't say something positive, don't say anything at all." "Your feelings aren't important." "Keep your opinions to yourself." "If you're going to be angry, this conversation is over." "Don't be such a baby." We've all heard sentences like these at some point in our life. They once had the power to make us feel alone and foolish. They will do the very same thing now if we keep obeying them.

Ask yourself these questions: What old, discouraging messages about the value of your ideas, experiences, beliefs, and feelings are keeping you feeling alone and separate from your partner? How many times do you stop yourself from speaking up, only to feel frustrated or resentful? Is it possible that *you* are sending *new* messages that discourage your partner from putting down his/her masks?

Trying Not to Be a Burden

◆ *Brenda won't tell her partner that she is having trouble handling her credit card debts because she knows that he has a hard time dealing with money issues and Brenda doesn't want to stress him out.*

◆ *Anton won't tell his partner that he has a small benign tumor on his foot that is going to require surgery because his partner is coping with her father's illness right now and Anton doesn't want to add to her emotional burden.*

◆ *Olivia won't tell her husband that his mother talks to her disrespectfully because she doesn't want to make him feel pressured to confront her and have an ugly scene.*

Many of us keep information from our partners because we feel "It's too much for them" or "It isn't a good time." But these are usually one-sided decisions, made without direct input, that may or may not be wise. How would you feel if you learned that your partner was keeping important personal information from you because he/she didn't want to "be a burden"? Aren't those decisions something we want to be a part of? *When we act like caretakers in a relationship we think we are doing the kind and noble thing, but sometimes our decisions keep our partner disconnected from us, and at a distance.*

Ask yourself: How might your attempts to "not be a burden" be sabotaging the emotional connection in your relationship?

Afraid to Rock the Boat

◆ *Jasper is afraid to tell his girlfriend he doesn't really like Indian food.*

◆ *Samantha is afraid to tell her fiancé she is tired of his cologne.*

◆ *Alicia is afraid to tell her partner that she thinks he relies too much on alcohol to have a good time.*

◆ *Belinda is afraid to say no to her husband's constant sexual advances, so she ends up having sex at least four nights a week and hating it half of the time.*

◆ *Todd doesn't want Janet to know that his mother has been hospitalized and takes medications for manic depressive behavior.*

Some of these issues may seem small, while others are clearly large, but all of them interfere with the process of intimate connection. I know that when a relationship is, for the most part, "working," it can be very hard to introduce new information. The fear, of course, is that this new information is going to change the relationship for the worse, or even destroy it. Yet trying to protect the status quo in a relationship by wearing an agreeable mask is the easiest way to kill the growth of a partnership. *The evolution of an effective partnership relies*

on the constant introduction of new information. You are always changing as a person, and you need to incorporate these changes into the
partnership. While this is a *slow*, step-by-step process, it is a necessary
process. Your growth, your new insights, your new observations, and
your ever-changing feelings are nourishment for the relationship.
Some of this "food" will not be easy for you and/or your partner to
digest, but it is the very stuff that keeps a relationship vital and on the
growth track. Keeping this food away from your partner to preserve
the relationship is self-defeating.

Consider these questions: What agreeable masks are you wearing right now in your relationship because it feels too risky to rock the
boat? Can you see how your attempts to preserve the status quo may
actually be jeopardizing your connection?

Trying to Be Who (We Think)
Our Partner Wants Us to Be

◆ *Janine feels she is failing as a partner if she can't always be bub-
bly, enthusiastic, and "up." She would be shocked to learn that her
partner often wishes Janine wasn't "on" all of the time.*

◆ *Frederick feels he is failing as a partner if he can't always be the
"understanding" one who is ready to offer wise counsel. He would
be shocked to learn that his partner wishes Frederick would have
his helpless moments too, and turn to her more for help.*

Many of us create a false persona that we bring into our romantic
relationships, but as the relationship starts to evolve, we don't know
how to dismantle that persona. We become a prisoner of our own creation, especially when we think that this persona is who our partner
wants us to be. Frederick and Janine have defined their value around
their masks. Both are certain they are giving their partners what they
need and want most. If a certain role has worked for you in the world,
it is easy to assume it will work in your partnership. Perhaps you think

it is what makes you interesting or desirable. But the goal of each individual in a partnership is *not* to be the most perfect version of who you think your partner wants you to be. ***The goal of partnership is to be the fullest expression of who you really are.*** And a loving partner will appreciate and support that goal.

Trying to Hide Our Imperfections

Vera will not undress in front of her partner unless the room is dark because she hates the shape of her thighs. She won't wear open toe sandals because she thinks her toes are ugly. And she would never leave the house—not even to walk the dog—without wearing makeup. Vera thinks she is preserving her allure and desirability, but her partner doesn't agree. He feels Vera judges herself too harshly, and he sometimes wonders if she is judging him this harshly.

It is hard to live in a culture that glorifies perfection—be it the perfect body, the perfect car, the perfect house, the perfect job, or the perfect chocolate soufflé. ***When the quest for perfection makes us feel ashamed of who we are, what we look like, what we do, and what we have, partnership can suffer.*** How perfect do you need to be for your partner right now to feel that you are lovable?

Consider these three questions: What less-than-perfect parts of you do you insist on hiding? How might your lack of self-acceptance be creating discomfort for your partner? How might it be a silent source of resentment and/or anger for *you*? Now think about the freedom you would feel if you could let your masks of perfection down.

Trying to Be of One Mind

◆ *Whenever Nadia wants to listen to music, she always picks a CD she knows her partner will like because she thinks it is important that they enjoy the same music.*

◆ *Whenever Alexander and his girlfriend go to the video store, he always lets her pick the movies because he doesn't want their choices to conflict.*

When a relationship is new and intense, there can be so much agreement between partners that it can genuinely feel, at times, as though you are both "of one mind." You like the same food, you like the same music, you like doing the same things and going to the same places. You go to sleep together, you wake up together, and you are in perfect agreement about where to set the thermostat and what food to keep in the refrigerator. But as the relationship settles in and both partners start gearing up for the longer haul, differences start to surface. When these differences surface, some of us scurry to conceal them. We eat things we don't want to eat, go to bed when we're not tired, spend time doing activities we don't enjoy, and so on, because we think we have to stay completely in synch with our partners. This can be a big mistake, particularly when concealing differences builds resentment. *Differences are a healthy sign that the relationship is EVOLVING, not dissolving. Differences should be celebrated, not buried.*

Ask yourself: What differences are you hiding from your partner right now because you're afraid to not be in perfect synch? How might you be subtly encouraging your partner to conceal his/her differences?

FEAR KEEPS MOST OF OUR MASKS IN PLACE

Look once more at the various mechanisms that encourage us to keep our masks in place. There is one common thread running through most of these mechanisms: the fear of rejection and/or abandonment. Can you see this in your own behavior? Let's face it—if we weren't so afraid of being rejected, we would not be so vested in our masks. Our masks are our armor, something we have developed in response to a personal history of rejection and abandonment. They make us feel safe; they make us feel as though we will never be hurt again.

Out in the larger world, where too much intimacy may be inappropriate, unprotective, or unwelcome, masks have a real value. But wearing all of your masks in your most intimate settings creates a firm barrier to intimate connection that is hard to penetrate. Over time, this becomes a relationship problem. The longer we wear our masks in a relationship, the more likely we are to *become* those masks. Trying to protect ourselves, we actually *abandon* ourselves. Let me say that again: We abandon ourselves. We create, on our own, the very thing we fear most in others. And this completely limits our ability to make a genuinely loving connection.

The point here is that your masks aren't just keeping your partner at a distance. They can keep you at a distance from yourself, leaving you feeling empty, angry, and disconnected. There is just no way to "play it safe" in a relationship—not if your goal is a loving, effective partnership. You can't play it safe if you're playing for keeps. While I realize that this is not the best piece of news for many people, I also know too well that it is a crucial partnership paradigm.

BRINGING YOUR PARTNER INTO YOUR WORLD

Some of our masks are obvious, and some are subtle. Some are flimsy, and some are so effective and comfortable we can start to believe they are genuine. But every mask interferes with our goal for a more effective partnership. If a lasting, loving partnership is your sincere goal, you must begin the slow, and very scary process of lowering your masks. And you must also encourage your partner to do the same. But how do you start such a daunting task?

When my relationship with Jill started to get serious, I realized that I was always going to feel separate if I kept the details of my life separate. Having been a single man for so many years, I was very comfortable keeping lots of information to myself, and it didn't feel strange or inappropriate to me. I was used to managing my ups and downs, working through my own personal and professional problems, celebrating my small successes by myself, and basically taking care of myself.

While I was sincerely interested in being incorporated into Jill's world, it was hard for me to believe that the events of my day and my life were something Jill wanted or needed to hear. Jill would ask, "How was your day?" and I would answer her with a simple, "Fine"—even if I had spent half the day on the telephone fighting with the cable company. Jill would ask, "How is your work going?" and I would answer quite cheerily, "Fine"—even if I had been loathing my work for weeks and agonizing over every paragraph. Jill would ask, "How is your family?" after noticing that I was talking to them on the phone, and I would answer "Fine"—even if they were making me completely nuts.

It probably doesn't surprise you to learn that a combination of skepticism and old, entrenched behavior kept me feeling strangely "single" long after Jill and I were an established couple. Eventually, however, with much support and encouragement from Jill, this is where I started my "mask-lowering" journey; it is where you might consider starting yours.

It did not take long for me to discover that the things you feel every day, see every day, worry about every day, and wonder about every day are a significant part of the relationship matrix. The argument you had with your boss. The hysterical phone call from your mother. The funny letter you just received from your college roommate. The new hiding spot that your cat just discovered. The weird noise that your car makes every time you put it in reverse. The message on your answering machine that made you smile. The great shirt you found in a bargain bin at the mall. The strange feeling of sadness that hit you in the middle of the day. These are the things that make up your life. Sharing your life means regularly sharing these pieces. It's like constantly tying little knots between you and your partner—knots that, over time, create a complex and resilient fabric of connectedness. It may feel like a small and subtle process, but it is actually a *primary* way of creating an ongoing feeling of connection and partnership.

For years and years I kept these moments to myself and I kept these feelings to myself. I was a "collector" who kept everything inside because I didn't know any better. But today I understand that what my wife appreciates most is my willingness to let her into my world on a daily basis, and my eagerness to become more a part of her world every day. It is when I *don't* let her in that she gets genuinely upset.

FEELING SPLIT IN HALF BY "INTERNAL CENSORS"

Part of the problem with wearing many relationship masks is that the masks keep splitting you in half. Instead of being one healthy individual with one clear voice, you wind up being two people: the person you know, and the person you let your partner know. This splitting mechanism is driven by what I call your *"internal censor."* And it does not support your goals for a loving, long-term partnership.

Every time you make the decision to withhold facts or feelings from your partner, your internal censor is hard at work. *Let me give you some examples:*

- If you're thinking, "I'm too tired to go out tonight," but you tell your partner, "Let's go," your censor is hard at work.
- If you're worrying that your new job is in jeopardy but you're telling your partner, "Everything's great," your censor is hard at work.
- If you're thinking, "I don't agree with what you're saying," but you're nodding your head in agreement, your censor is hard at work.
- If you're thinking, "I really hate that," but you're saying to

your partner, "I don't care," your censor is hard at work.

- If you're thinking, "That really hurts my feelings," but you're not saying a single word, your censor is working overtime.

When your inner dialogue (the ongoing conversation you have only with yourself) is not in accord with your outer relationship dialogue (the things you say to your partner) your relationship can pay the price.

The internal censor isn't just about words and feelings. It can affect your behavior, too. For example:

- If you snack all day long in private so you can give the appearance of being a light eater when you have dinner with your partner, your censor is hard at work.
- If your in-laws are driving your crazy, but you're all smiles whenever you see them or talk about them, your censor is hard at work.
- If you're hiding the phone bills every month because you don't want your partner to know how much time you spend talking to your mother, your censor is hard at work.

When your inner experience is not in accord with your outer relationship behavior, it is your relationship, once again, that can pay the price.

INTERNAL CENSORS VS. "HEALTHY ALIGNMENT"

Some of us are so used to feeling split in half that we don't even realize how angry this constant censoring process makes us feel. But it *does* make us angry. And frustrated. And resentful. And it keeps us feeling very separate from our partner.

One of your primary relationship goals, starting today, should be creating something I call *"healthy alignment."* Healthy alignment means being more willing to say and do things that genuinely reflect how you feel, what you need, and who you are. Healthy alignment means being able to choose honesty over political correctness. Healthy alignment means being willing to risk disagreement. Healthy alignment means doing less caretaking. Healthy alignment means being able to say more of what is on your mind. Healthy alignment means being able to risk greater visibility in the relationship. Healthy alignment means being able to take better care of yourself. Healthy alignment means not feeling split in half.

Healthy alignment can feel very different than what you are used to, and it can certainly feel risky at times. But it is a powerful antidote to the toxic effects of masks, and it makes the relationship soil fertile for genuine partnership. You are not an automobile, and it is going to take more than one hour in the shop to bring your many parts into full alignment. It may take months, or even years, happening only one small step a time. But the idea of being in healthy alignment is an image you should always have in your mind, and a feeling you should be constantly striving to create and maintain.

Finding the Words and Actions That Bring You into Alignment

Let's take a second look at some of the censoring scenarios I just gave as examples and see how you might start the challenging process of dismantling some of your masks and creating a more healthy alignment without starting a firefight.

Example 1: You're thinking, "I'm too tired to go out tonight." Instead of telling your partner "Let's go," you might say, "I'm certainly happy to go if this is important to you, but I need to tell you before we go that I'm terribly tired." Maybe going out isn't that important to your partner. And if it is, you don't have to make believe that you're not exhausted.

Take Off the Masks

Example 2: You're worried that your new job is in jeopardy. When your partner asks you how your new job is going, you might say, "Frankly, it's a little confusing right now." This opens the door to talking more about your concerns without scaring your partner unnecessarily.

Example 3: You're thinking "I don't agree with what you're saying." Instead of nodding your head, you might say, "What you say is interesting, though I must admit that I have a different opinion." This establishes your strength without cutting down your partner.

Example 4: You're thinking "That really hurts my feelings." Instead of being silent, try something simple, honest, and direct such as, "Ouch . . . ," said in a very matter-of-fact voice. A response like this is disarming; it communicates clearly and it facilitates discussion, apologies, and healing because it is not an attack.

Example 5: Your in-laws are driving you crazy. If they're not giving you something to smile about, *take that smile off your face.* You can be respectful without being cheery and dishonest about the way you feel. Your lack of enthusiasm sends an important message to your in-laws *and* your partner.

Example 6: You're hiding the phone bill because you're afraid your partner is going to scrutinize the calls you make to your mother. If you feel this behavior is unhealthy, hiding the bills only keeps it unhealthy. If, on the other hand, your partner is envious or judgmental of this telephone relationship, it may be something he/she needs to examine more carefully. Use the phone bill to help start a dialog.

Can you think of some appropriate words and actions that will start to bring you into a more healthy alignment?

SEPARATION STARTS WITH A
SINGLE STEP; JOINING DOES, TOO

Taking off the masks is an ongoing process, not a one-time event. It took many years for most of these masks to be created, and it is unreasonable to expect that you can undo them all in the blink of an eye. That shouldn't be your goal. The idea is to get started—to get started right now. Every single day presents you with opportunities to challenge your masks and create something more real. Maybe it will require a bit of new language, or maybe it will require a bit of new behavior. Maybe it will be a little scary, or maybe it will be surprisingly easy. Half the work, in my opinion, is clearly identifying those masks and understanding how and why they have come to exist. As I've said already, many of our masks have been on so long they feel like our real skin. But they aren't. And the more you are aware of their presence, the more uncomfortable they start to feel.

The other half of the work is all about trust. Lowering masks, for the most part, means taking risks. "How will my partner react?" "How will this change the relationship?" "How will this change *me*?" These are not easy questions. Yet every time a mask is lowered—even just a few inches—and we survive the process, we are building trust. Trust is something that *has* to be built. It is never a given, not even in the most ideal relationships. And that construction happens in the smallest of increments. Lowering the masks, one step at a time, is one of the most powerful ways that we can feel our trust grow.

Every day we wear our masks in the presence of the one we love we move a little further way from a true partnership, and we feel a little more separate and alone. But every time we challenge our masks we feel progress in our relationship. We feel a change in the connection. Even the smallest step in the right direction feels like a victory for your partnership. *As you take these courageous steps, keep the following guidelines in mind:*

Ask Yourself Revealing Questions

Taking down the masks means constantly asking yourself these important questions: "Where am I not being honest right now?" "Where am I not being real?" "Where am I not being true to myself?" "Where am I not being true to my partner?" "When I sacrifice authenticity for the sake of the relationship, how does this sacrifice backfire—does it make me feel angry? depressed? cheated? alone?" "How are my masks sabotaging my hopes for real partnership?" I still ask myself these questions regularly, and I would encourage you to do the same. Then let your answers steer you in a healthier new direction.

Try to Understand Your Masks Before You Start Taking Them Down

Every mask exists for a reason, and the clearer you are about each reason the easier it will be to dismantle each mask. Try to understand the history of your many masks. Is the mask an old friend, or is it something you have recently created? What purpose did it serve when you first put it on? Is it still serving that purpose now? Imagine what it would feel like to be rid of the mask, and pay attention to the many complex feelings this triggers. The more you understand the origins of each mask, the less likely you are to put it back on. Consciousness is liberating.

Take Your Fears Seriously

Some masks feel as though they are Krazy-Glued to your soul. That glue is made of fear, and you need to take that fear seriously. Not every mask is easily shed, and the last masks to come off are the ones that are terror-driven. Taking down these masks can require months or years of hard work and ongoing risk-taking. Often, we need help from friends, family, counselors, therapists, *and*, ultimately, our partner. It's all part of the process.

Make Healthy Alignment Your Goal

Sometimes it takes a lot of experimentation to get things right. Give yourself the chance to "try on" different language and different behavior. If it doesn't feel *authentic*—if you don't like the way that new language or behavior fits you—try on other language and behavior. Keep experimenting until you find that "natural fit" that I call healthy alignment.

Don't Expect to Be Perfect

Taking down the masks, for most of us, is a challenging, ongoing process. Our goal is to make *progress*, not to reach perfection. Every bit of progress you make is rewarded with a more genuine sense of loving connection and partnership. Expecting perfection keeps the masks from coming down. After all, perfection is also a mask.

SECRET #3:

Make "We" a Priority

. ◆ .

First eyes meet. Then hearts meet. And soon, there is "a couple." Two individuals quite separate and distinct, and sometimes from two very different worlds, now face the task of creating something larger—a place of shared experience, shared beliefs, shared feelings, shared goals, shared space, and often, shared finances. None of this is necessarily easy or natural. Yet it is fundamental to the experience of "joining." And that process of two people joining into partnership revolves around the word "we."

You may have a completely loving heart and sincere intentions, but if you have spent years being single, most likely you will enter into the most committed relationship still thinking, feeling, and acting in the "I." This, by the way, is appropriate in the very beginning of a relationship, and this is healthy. But what happens next?

While many couples are partnered in bed, partnered in their living arrangements, and partnered on paper, they remain uncoupled in most of their thoughts, feelings, and actions. They have gone through the motions of becoming a "we", but they still think mostly in the "I," speak mostly in the "I," and behave mostly in the "I." I know people

65

who have been married for years, who acknowledge that they still have problems thinking of themselves as being part of a couple. In short, "we" does not happen in a single moment of bliss or in an afternoon of religious ceremony.

"We" is more than a simple two-letter word. It is the bridge between two individuals—both the symbol and the substance of true connection. Thinking as part of a bigger entity has to be learned. A "we" has to grow, and it has to build strength not just on paper, but deep in the heart. *Building a partnership is a never-ending process of building the shared experience called "we."*

LEARNING "WE" LANGUAGE: THE FIRST PARTNERSHIP LESSON

I still remember the earliest stages of transition in my relationship from being an "I" to being part of a "we." For me, the change began in my use of "we" language. A close friend would ask me, "What are you doing tonight?" And while half of me was still thinking, "*I'm* not really doing anything . . ." I would consciously stop myself from offering that answer (sometimes, quite forcefully). And then, instead, I would say, "*We're* not really doing anything," or "I'm not sure . . . I have to talk to Jill." *This was not natural for me.* And it was not easy. I had been single for forty years of my life. Being suddenly partnered did not automatically ensure a sudden and complete shift in my words, in my thoughts, or in my actions.

For me, learning and practicing "we" language was the best place to start my ascent into partnership. I feel that this is a good place for *most* people to start.

When two people make the decision to be together, often one of their first, and most special moments, is putting that joint message on the telephone answering machine. This is a real "we" language moment. But one message on the answering machine does not a relationship make. Learning "we" language means learning to substitute certain "*single words*" in your vocabulary for "*partnership words*." And the process is ongoing. Here are the "single words" you want to be noticing most: *I, me, my,* and *mine.* And here are the "partnership words" you want to be building into your sentences: *we, us, our.*

"We," "us," and "our" are words that *both* partners need to say and hear again and again and again and again. I am not suggesting that "your" sandwich has to become "our" sandwich, or that "your" socks have to become "our" socks. Clearly, there are many things that are supposed to remain separate. But the appropriate and consistent use of "we," "us," and "our" is a behavior modification technique that is as powerful as it is simple. These words are partnership glue.

"WE" LANGUAGE BREAKS THROUGH THE BARRIERS

The resistance to becoming "we" is built out of years of separateness and lots of *fear.* Learning and practicing "we" language slowly but firmly breaks through both of those obstacles, giving you the opportunity to begin *feeling* more joined. "We" language—even the simplest sentences—touches your own heart every bit as much as it touches the heart of your partner.

- "We" language tells your partner that you are feeling more coupled than single.
- "We" language tells the world (friends, family, etc.) that you are feeling more coupled than single.
- "We" language reinforces your own internal experience of feeling more coupled than single.

Let me illustrate . . .

Example 1: It's dinnertime. Note the difference between saying "*I want pizza tonight*" and saying, "What should *we* get for dinner?" *One focuses on the individual; the other acknowledges the couple.*

Example 2: You can't find the teapot. Note the difference between saying, "Where did you put *my* teapot?" and saying, "Where did you put *our* teapot?" *One separates possessions; the other celebrates sharing.*

Example 3: A friend asks you if you have plans for the evening. Note the difference between saying, "*I'm* busy tonight" and saying, "*We're* busy tonight." *One is self-involved; the other presents a united front.*

Example 4: Someone asks you how long you have been married. Note the difference between saying, "*I've* been married five years" and saying "*We've* been married five years." *One makes the experience seem singular; the other makes it clear that you feel you are part of a couple.*

Can you see the difference in each of these examples? Can you see how the "we" (partnership) words conveys a more inclusive message than the "I" (single) words? Sometimes it is subtle, and sometimes it is not subtle at all. But the message is going out—it's going out to your partner, to your friends, to your family, to the world. And the message is also going *in*—deep inside your emotional world—shaping and reinforcing your experience of being coupled.

BUILDING PARTNERSHIP FROM THE OUTSIDE, IN

Learning to speak in the "we" is, admittedly, an "outside-in" approach to emotional growth, letting the words do a lot of the work. But that doesn't make it dishonest or ineffective. It's actually quite the opposite. When the relationship, no matter how committed, is new enough so that you still *feel* single and separate in many ways, an outside-in approach is powerful and meaningful. And sometimes, particularly if you are very defended and self-protective, as I was, it's your only easy choice.

Make "We" a Priority

Let's face it. Sometimes you have to "dress up" like a partner before you can genuinely feel the part. You shouldn't be ashamed of that—many of us go through this phase when we are struggling to build a lasting relationship. And that is where "we" language comes in. Learning to speak in the "we" isn't about training yourself to say the *right*, politically correct, relationship thing. It's about giving yourself a chance to try on a new identity with your language and giving those words a chance to sink in and penetrate.

Speaking in the "we" opens the door to *feeling* more "we." As this feeling builds, it isn't long before the "we" words start coming from the inside-out. It's almost magical how much power these words have to affect your heart.

Making "We" Language Your Daily Language

Partnership grows one "we" at a time. This is why you should be looking for daily opportunities to insert partnership language into your vocabulary.

Here's one simple goal that you can easily achieve: Make a commitment to using the word "we" just one more time each day than you do right now. One more time. Starting today. Try to do this in the *beginning* of the day, not as an afterthought at the end of the day. Force it into one of your sentences if you have to, but do it. No day should go by without a single "we." *This is your one-a-day partnership vitamin.*

Your once-a-day "we" guarantees at least one important, daily experience of feeling more bound as a couple. It tends to start the flow of "we" language for the rest of the day, setting a tone of togetherness that can carry forward through your words and your partner's words. It gives everyone permission to leave the more protective single state and access the riskier partnered state. This may sound very simple, but there is nothing simple about the experience it creates.

THIS IS HOW LOVE WORKS

Harnessing the Power of Your Partner's Name

When we are away from our partners for many hours of the day, which is unavoidable for most of us, it is easy to slip into a more "separated" mode as we interact with friends, co-workers, and the many individuals who make up our daily world. Yet being physically disconnected can lead to disconnected language. There are, however, ways to combat this "out of sight, out of mind" experience, and one of the most effective ways is with "we" language.

Here is another simple, daily goal: When you and your partner are apart, *use your partner's name* in a sentence, at least once-a-day, during the many conversations you have with friends, family, co-workers, etc. I'm talking about simple phrases such as: "Amy would enjoy this . . . ," "Jack had an experience like that . . . ," "I'll have to tell that to Joan. . . ." Insert it into your conversation, even if you have to force it. Avoid distancing words and phrases such as "my significant other" and "you know who. . . ." Use your partner's *name*. Incorporate it into your reality, and let that name be your bridge back to your feelings.

The simple mention of your partner's name, in their absence, is enough to conjure up their spirit and bring them into the room with you like relationship voodoo. It says to others, "I am partnered." More important, it conveys the same message to the person who needs to hear it most: you.

BRINGING YOUR "WE" INTO THE WORLD

Katrina and Edward have been together for over a year, yet Edward still distrusts the relationship and questions its future. At the heart of Edward's distrust is the complex nature of Katrina's romantic behavior. When Katrina and Edward are together alone, Katrina can be absolutely lovey-dovey. She can be very affectionate and extremely sexual. Yet as soon as they walk out the front door into the world, Katrina gets annoyed if Edward tries to hold her hand.

Make "We" a Priority

In the many years I spent observing, dissecting, and writing about commitment conflict, I was always encountering "loving" couples who did not seem very loving as they moved through the world. While comfortable with being intensely intimate behind closed doors, there was little or no evidence of their connection in front of those doors. There was no affectionate touching. And the physical distance between the two could be measured with yardsticks. There was no missing the fact that one or both partners was not ready to say to the world, "We are a couple."

Out at the Movies, Building "We"

About a year ago at a party I had separate conversations with a man and a woman who my friend, the hostess, later told me were a married couple. I was completely surprised. Nothing about their behavior toward each other that entire evening indicated they even knew each other. When I voiced my surprise, my friend said that I was not the only one that evening who had this reaction. Six months after that party, my friend told me that the couple had split up. She said that this was one breakup that surprised no one.

How does *your* physical behavior say to your partner, and to the world, "We are a couple."? *Think about some of these things:*

- How often do you reach out, spontaneously, to take your partner's hand?
- How often do you hold hands or touch when you are at a restaurant, a friend's house, or at a party?
- Do you ever kiss your partner hello or goodbye in public?
- Do you touch or hold hands when you're at the movies, a concert, a ballgame, a picnic?
- Do you walk down the street like you are part of a couple, fully conscious of the physical space between you? Does it

feel as though you are connected with a rubber band that can only stretch so far?

- Or do you fail what a friend of mine calls the "walking-down-the-street test" because you are out of synch and easily separated?
- Is your body language still screaming "single" even though you have long been part of a couple?

I am not advocating giant public displays of affection here. I don't enjoy watching couples slurp each other's faces on street corners any more than you do. And I respect people who are only comfortable with a genteel, restrained public expression of their affection. But I also find it painful to watch couples who cannot bring their connection into the world with a single physical gesture. These simple gestures are one of the most effective ways to counter the natural "drifting apart" that most couples experience when they are out in the world. And the ability to keep intimacy in a small box, away from the larger world, is not a healthy trait.

Being More Conscious of Your Body's "We" Messages

About a year after Jill and I were married, Jill made it clear to me how some of my social skills were still rooted in the single world. It seems that every time we were at a party together I would move to her side during our conversations and talk to her as we both looked out into the room. Finally, one day she just said to me, "Why can't you stay in front of me, face me head on, and turn your back to the party?" I was completely stumped by this question. I thought our casual, side-by-side "observer" stance was as comfortable for her as it was for me. I know how much we enjoyed sharing our various observations during an evening. And we were certainly not disconnected. I had to recognize, however, that a lifetime of being single, and worse, being an observer of relationship behavior, had locked me into this side-by-side viewing position. I felt uncomfortable turning this observer off. Yet my stance made my wife feel like less of a couple, and this was something I had to become conscious of.

Sometimes expressing more "we" when you are out in the world with your partner just requires more awareness. You may think you're doing a great job, but you can have huge blindspots in your language and gestures, giving your partner a very different experience. Basic awareness can quickly lead to positive change, particularly because it requires so little energy to make these changes once you become aware of your blind spots.

For others more entrenched in the "I," incorporating "we" into body language and gestures is a more complex "re-education" process. Awareness still comes first, but that must be followed by a lot of conscious practice. With conscious practice, "we" gestures and "we" language work their way from the outside, in, slowly breaking down internal resistance and old "I" patterns. Even if this feels somewhat unnatural at first, over time these gestures and this language become a completely natural part of who you are on the inside. Repetition creates a new reality.

Being conscious of how you physically bring an expression of "we" out of your house and into the world is a critical part of "we" building.

Surviving "We" Envy

"We" gestures and "we" language can create some genuine "we" envy. Many of us have been working overtime to protect friends, family, and others from seeing the true "we" that we feel in our loving relationship. We're afraid to alienate those we have been close to in the past, fracture old alliances, create discomfort, invite jealousy, criticism, and other negativity. We protect everyone but our partners.

You can't hide the "we" in your heart to caretake other people in your world. *Either you are going to be a couple or you are NOT going to be a couple; there is no safe in-between.* Good friends and acquaintances and genuinely caring family members *will* survive a shift in your behavior because they want to survive the shift that is taking place in your life. Roles may change, but that is not the end of the world. On the other hand, there will be some people who, for whatever reason, have no room in their lives for this new entity that you and your partner are building. Sometimes building "we" means letting go of old connections.

Surviving "We" Terror

Creating a partnership that has substance and meaning is a challenge for *all* men and women, however well-intentioned. "We" envy is certainly a part of that challenge. Long-established, deeply rooted, extremely comfortable, single "me" habits are a bigger part of that challenge. But let us not forget about the silent menace: "we" terror.

It is really important for each and every one of us who desires greater intimacy to acknowledge just how scary it is to exchange the safer, more predictable, more controllable state of "I" for a riskier, less predictable, less controllable, genuine feeling of "we." In our heart of hearts, many of us cling to the notion that we have less to lose by staying emotionally separate. To join more fully in a partnership is to invite *both* love and loss. And this makes it incredibly hard to say even the simplest "we" statements or make even the most subtle "we" gestures. The desire may be there, but we're just not quite ready to open that door.

Yet as long as that door stays closed, the most rewarding kind of partnership remains beyond your grasp. If you are losing the battle to utter simple "we" language and to offer your partner the kinds of simple gestures that show your desire to present a "we" to the world, this might be the time to consider seeking professional assistance from a skilled therapist or counselor. In my experience—professional *and* personal—much of the terror that seems insurmountable is far less overwhelming once it is intelligently and compassionately deconstructed.

It may not be the easiest process, but it is a liberating one. *Building a stronger "we" means confronting our fears of losing that "we."*

HOME ALONE, STUCK IN THE "I"

Elanor is home in bed with a 102° fever and a serious case of the flu. Richie, Elanor's partner, is freaking out. Richie is not freaking out because Elanor is ill—he is freaking out because Elanor has shut him out of her world. When Elanor gets sick, she completely retreats into the "I." She doesn't let Richie take her to the doctor. She doesn't let Richie get her stuff at the pharmacy. She doesn't let Richie make her soup. And she snarls when Richie tries to talk to her. When Elanor gets sick, she wants to be alone and miserable, and it doesn't matter to her that she's been in a relationship with Richie for five years. Not surprisingly, this makes Richie pretty miserable, too, and it leaves him feeling confused and uncoupled.

Many of us have personal triggers that have us retreating into the "I." Physical illness, financial stress, and job traumas are three common triggers. In our distress—in those times when we need help *most*—we can "forget" that we have a partner. We feel isolated, unable or unwilling to reach out to our partners for help. Typically, we are so lost in our own distress that we don't even consider how this might be affecting our partner or our relationship.

When Elanor is sick she regresses to the many times when she was sick as a child and her mother, who had a full-time job, could not be home all day to take care of her. As a child, Elanor decided that she couldn't count on anyone but herself. She is still angry about those times, and today, as an adult, her anger shows in her defiant attitude towards anyone who offers her care. The problem is that Elanor has a partner who *does* care, and who *can* help. Her inability to let that new reality into her world reinforces the "I" at the expense of the "we."

Like Elanor, we all have very good reasons for retreating into the "I." But the only way to build a strong partnership that can be trust-

75

ed is to challenge those reasons and take the risk of reaching out for support. These are the moments when you must *force* yourself to think more in the "we." Loving relationships are not just about sharing the good times. Sharing your struggles is one of the most important parts of building and fortifying your sense of partnership.

CREATING "WE" SPACE

In some relationships, one of the first things both partners do is give up their old "single" living situations and find a new apartment or house. But this is not always possible. Far more often, financial issues, emotional issues, timing problems, and the cruel realities of the real estate market make it necessary for us to convert one partner's "single" living space into a shared, "coupled" space. When these mergers happen, it is not always easy to create a new and genuinely balanced "we" space.

If you gave up your space to move into his or her space, are you still feeling like an unwelcome guest? Are you afraid to challenge the status quo? Are you afraid to speak up for certain needs you might have (like a firmer mattress, a different shower head, a larger refrigerator, more shelf space for your books)? Are you afraid to recreate the living environment into something that expresses a partnership? Think about how your discomfort and your one-sided compromising may be keeping you from feeling more connected to your partner.

If your special "single" space is now home for two people, are there any resentments or regrets you are containing just beneath the surface? Are you unwilling to give up your dishes, towels, linens, and decor to create a new expression of partnership? Does a part of you really miss having a space you didn't have to share? Try to honestly inventory the ways you may be making statements in your space that say: "We are together, but we still aren't truly partnered."

For the first eight months Jill and I lived together, we were sharing a little house—*her* little house—which had to become "our" little house. This was very difficult for both of us, even though Jill was incredibly generous with her willingness to place many of her things in storage in order to incorporate some of my things, as well as various new "we" things. Even when we were finally able to move to an apartment that *we* found together, we both still wrestled with space issues. This stuff is hard. The mistake is making-believe it is *not* hard.

Creating a "we" space is—practically speaking—one of the most comprehensive challenges of a new partnership. Both partners have to be willing to sacrifice a lot of "I" for the sake of "we." There is no magic formula for this. And it does not sort itself out overnight. But during the many rounds of discussion, negotiation, argument, sacrifice, and compromise that cannot be avoided, the word that will lead you to your best, most hopeful solutions is the two-letter word *we*. *Being together means creating a space that is "OURS." Our* apartment. *Our* house. *Our* home. You might have separate bathrooms, separate closets, and separate home offices (if you're lucky enough to have enough space), but the overriding feeling has to become a unified feeling of "we." The more this feeling is evident in your words, your thoughts, and your actions, the better the prognosis for a successful transition. Holding on to the "my" in "This used to be *my* house" is how individuals hold on to their separateness.

PUTTING THE RELATIONSHIP FIRST

When we set out to build a future with a partner we love, the organizing theme is "we." We share families, children, friends, money, houses, vacations, and decisions. We often feel the same feelings, and we sometimes even experience the same fears. The challenge, always, is to never lose track of the "we," and to remember that the strongest sense of "we" is the "we" that we build in the heart.

THIS IS HOW LOVE WORKS

Making "We" Decisions

Deidre and Bobby are having an uncomfortable relationship moment. Earlier this afternoon, one of Deidre's girlfriends asked if she and Bobby could join her and her husband on Friday for an early dinner at one of their favorite restaurants—early because this other couple has a babysitter who can't stay out late. Deidre quickly accepted, and, later in the day, casually mentioned this to Bobby. About ten minutes ago, Bobby realized exactly why he is feeling so annoyed; he has just said to Deidre: "You know how stressful it is for me to quit work early. . . . Would you please ask me first next time before you agree to make a plan like that?"

Deidre would never want to intentionally add to Bobby's stress load. Yet this has happened anyway, because her "me" reflex made a quick decision. This is not an unusual thing to happen between members of a loving couple, but it does create a problem.

Stuart and Brittany, who live in San Francisco, have been together for almost eighteen months. Several weeks ago, Stuart learned that his company was downsizing and that his job would probably be ending shortly. Afraid of being jobless for any length of time, he immediately started sending off resumes. Because of the highly specialized nature of his work, Stuart knows that getting a new job in his field probably means relocating to another city. Yet Stuart hasn't wanted to talk a lot about this until he had a firm offer. "Why agonize about these things prematurely?" he tells himself. This week, Stuart received two offers—one in Dallas and one in San Jose— and tonight he asked Brittany, for the first time, how she feels about moving to Dallas. Brittany's immediate, very emotionally charged response was, "Why haven't you been discussing this possibility with me all along?"

Stuart never intended to make Brittany feel alienated from him. He hopes to marry Brittany next year, and he wants her to move with him wherever he chooses to relocate. But he has acted very "single" in response to his job crisis.

Make "We" a Priority

Decisions that affect both members of a couple are decisions best made by both members of the couple. Spending years without a good partnership hones your "me" skills in the decision-making department. At this point in your life, you are probably so skilled at making decisions—both small daily decisions and larger life decisions—that the process is almost automatic. But this is very anti-partnership. The only way to counter this is to take your brain off automatic pilot and keep reminding yourself that you have a co-pilot sitting next to you.

Letting Go of Certain "I" Behavior

Carla and Delon are in the middle of another argument about Delon's "I" behavior. One hour ago, Carla and Delon ordered dinner from their favorite Thai restaurant—a restaurant where Carla has lunch at least once a week. When the food they ordered didn't arrive after forty-five minutes Delon snatched the telephone, called the restaurant, and started arguing with the manager. "If you're short-staffed," he complained, "you should never have taken our order." Getting more agitated, he continued, "I think you should get in your car and deliver it to us yourself!" Carla is mortified. She feels she will never be able to eat in this restaurant again because Delon has made such a scene. Carla just wanted to know that their dinner was going to be delivered soon. Delon was not speaking for the couple when he spoke to the restaurant manager, and his need to "vent" has ruined Carla's evening and her appetite. "Why didn't you think about me before you started to tee off on this guy?" she asks Delon.

This whole unpleasant experience could have been avoided if Delon had simply had a short conversation with Carla before grabbing the phone and taking action—a conversation starting with the question, *"What should WE do about this?"* But Delon got completely caught up in his own frustration and his own anger and stopped acting like part of a couple. He stopped thinking about Carla's interests. He never considered asking for her opinion. He lost his connection to the "we." And he left Carla to feel less "coupled."

This kind of unpleasant drama is happening all the time in relationships, and it doesn't just happen in restaurants. Think about all of the people that you and your partner, as a couple, have some kind of relationship with. Your friends. Your neighbors. Your doctors, lawyers, accountants, and brokers. Your housekeeper and your babysitter. Your children's teachers. Your children's friends. And so on. Many of these relationships are critical, and your ability to interact with these people *as a couple* is essential. Yet way too often these important relationships are damaged or destroyed when one partner loses track of the "we."

It is very easy to lose your connection to the "we" when you get caught up in your own fear, frustration, anger, confusion, or passion. Then you start behaving "single," never considering the consequences of that behavior until later. These are the times when it is so important to come to a full stop, take a deep breath, and remind yourself that you are part of a couple now. How will your actions affect you *and* your partner? Is this what you *both* want? Are you sure? If you are not sure, protect your partnership by checking in with your partner before you take action. *Being in a loving partnership means understanding that what is best for ME is not always best for WE.*

My Stuff Becomes Our Stuff

Kenda is really angry at this moment. About fifteen minutes ago, seized by a mid-day hunger pang, she took a frozen pizza out of the freezer and put it in the oven to bake. Gordon, Kenda's fiancé, has just walked into the kitchen. He took one look at the pizza that had just come out of the oven and said: "You know, that was my pizza."

When we are in a loving relationship, some of us have an amazing ability to quickly turn over many of the simple "my" things we hold near and dear and make them "our" things. My television quickly becomes our television. My towels quickly become our towels. My music quickly becomes our music. My frozen pizza quickly becomes our frozen pizza.

Yet, for many more of us, this process of turning "my" things over to a larger "we" is not easy at all. Sometimes the transition takes a painfully long time, and sometimes the transition never comes. When that transition does not take place, we find ourselves with a partnership problem.

I am not saying that all personal boundaries have to melt into one communal "we." And I'm not talking here about personal stuff that is appropriately, or necessarily, separate. You are certainly entitled to have your own toothbrush, your own razor, and your own personal collection of fill-in-the-blank. *Your* diary is *your* diary. *Your* birthday present is *your* birthday present. *Your* teddy bear is *your* teddy bear. *Your* autographed Jackie Robinson baseball is *your* autographed Jackie Robinson baseball. But there is so much *other* stuff that needs to transition into the place of "we." And there is also the *new* stuff—stuff that you acquire once you are an established couple. While some of us can easily see the majority of these acquisitions as shared objects, others still assign single ownership (depending on who found it, who paid for it, etc.), maintaining a rigid division of "mine" and "yours." This rigid division maintains intense feelings of separateness.

It is worth noting here that some of our reluctance to become more "we" comes from a history of needing to fiercely defend the "mine." Some of us grew up feeling object-deprived and can't let go of our territorial instincts around the things we have struggled to acquire in our adult life. Some of us grew up in hotbeds of sibling warfare—sometimes overt, and sometimes hidden—that have us still acting like little kids who view sharing our stuff as a life-and-death struggle. I have seen men and women defend a handful of french fries from their respective partners the way one would defend a Ph.D. dissertation or a newborn baby. It can be, admittedly, quite amusing to witness. And it is all very understandable. Yet it is not conducive to loving feelings, and if you are hoping to move further down the partnership path, it is not at all constructive. Some of these old mechanisms need to be dismantled.

BAD STUFF IS "WE" STUFF, TOO, AND MOST PROBLEMS ARE "WE" PROBLEMS

Sometimes we can act very "we" around the positive things in our relationship, yet very "I" around the annoying, unpleasant, or difficult things. When his car breaks down, it's *his* problem. When the light-bulb in her closet burns out, it's *her* problem. When his brother is making him crazy, it's *his* brother. When her cousin is asking for money, it's *her* cousin. When he runs out of his favorite cereal, it's *his* cereal. When she gets an unfair parking ticket, it's *her* parking ticket. And so on.

One of the most valuable relationship lessons I learned early in my marriage was a lesson that revolved around unpleasant "we" stuff—the garbage, to be specific. It is a lesson worth sharing with you here.

Once a week I go into Jill's bathroom, empty her little wastebasket into a larger bag with the rest of the garbage, and take the garbage out of the house. I don't think twice about it. As far as I'm concerned, it is all *our* garbage. There is no separation—it just needs to be removed from the house once a week. Yet when I first started doing this, Jill was completely bowled over. Since the wastebasket was in her bathroom, she assumed that I would not be paying attention to it, or taking any responsibility for it. And the first time she saw that her wastebasket had been emptied, it touched her heart. Frankly, I think it still does.

Every single one of us has garbage we have to deal with—and not just the kind that fills little baskets. We have house garbage and work garbage and family garbage and friend garbage and an ongoing supply of miscellaneous life garbage. And the more we can learn to experience our garbage in the "we," the more we can genuinely feel that we are part of a partnership.

FINDING SPECIAL TIME FOR "WE"

While there are still twenty-four hours in every day of the week, time feels as though it is in painfully short supply these days. And while it is increasingly hard to find some personal time to take for ourselves, it is even harder to make time in our loving relationships for "we." Yet making time for "we" is an essential relationship requirement—it is relationship oxygen. Without that time together, the two members of a couple quickly start to feel like two separate satellites that bump into each other on rare, unpredictable occasions. And this feeling is, emotionally speaking, a painful one.

If it is partnership that you are looking for, you have to log partner hours. Not just a few minutes of so-called "quality time." This is why vacations are so vital. And why sometimes you have to give up your weekend golf game with your buddies. It's why staying home for a quiet evening together can be far more important than going out to an exciting party that will send you to separate corners of a room. It's why you can't always do the things you loved to do with your free time when you were single.

Making time for "we" means putting aside "I" wants and needs and making time for shared activity, even if that activity is hanging around the house doing nothing. It means doing things that are mutually agreed upon and mutually satisfying, even if those "things" are simple things like walking the dog together or going grocery shopping together. It means prioritizing the need to spend time in each other's physical presence, incorporating each other into your separate worlds.

Making time for "we" does not mean attaching yourselves at the hip. It means attaching yourselves through your attention to each other, your awareness of each other's presence, and your desire to feel more partnered. And it works its magic most when your eyes aren't on the clock.

TALKING $$$ IN THE "WE"

An old acquaintance of mine recently confided in me that she and her husband have not had a conversation about money for almost three years. "My husband has his way of dealing with money, I have mine, and we don't agree," she explained to me matter-of-factly, "so we keep everything completely separate and that's our solution." As I listened to this I became very uncomfortable. I am way too aware of how unrealistic it is to think that a couple can build togetherness while keeping financial matters 100 percent separate, and never talking about money.

How do two individuals who are both used to their financial independence start to deal with money in the "we"? Are each of us, as individuals, entitled to our own separate spending habits and decisions? Do all accounts have to merge? Are we supposed to take turns paying bills? Can we be frugal or reckless, as we individually choose? If I borrow money from my partner, do I have to pay my partner back? If my partner earns more money, should my partner be paying a larger share of the bills? These are all terribly difficult questions—questions that most couples wrestle with throughout the lifetime of their relationships.

It is quite common these days for two members of a couple to keep their money issues very "single," particularly in the early stages of a relationship. But as the relationship progresses (or perhaps, more accurately, *if* the relationship is to progress), it becomes critical that money develops into a "we" issue—an issue that both partners can, at the very least, *talk about* regularly, and, hopefully, find some middle ground. If there is no financial "we," the separation tends to create serious problems for long-term partnership.

Let me give you some examples . . .

Make "We" a Priority

◆ *Sasha is completely stressed out because she is on an incredibly tight budget. Her partner Alex is constantly spending money on his baseball memorabilia collection, but he won't offer more money towards the rent.*

◆ *Cindi is incredibly angry because she is always paying for the groceries and her partner Cal never asks her about this—and never offers to contribute.*

◆ *Bradford is unhappy because his wife is always sending money to her sister, and then always pleading poverty when their bills come.*

◆ *Vida is wigging out because the credit card collection agencies are calling the house constantly, looking for her boyfriend Bobby, yet every other week Bobby buys an expensive new tie for himself at Marshall Fields.*

◆ *Jonelle is feeling extraordinary pressure to spend money on vacations she can't afford because her partner Stephen says he needs to get away from New York City more often.*

There is little more complicated in relationships than finances. And I would never suggest that the only successful solution to money issues is a comprehensive merger where both partners must give up all financial separation for the good of the couple. After all, the old days and old ways of dealing with money—whether they were good or bad—are probably gone for good. But couples *have* to talk about money. They have to talk about money *constantly*. **Crucial money matters have to be discussed in the "we."**

Can we afford this? Do we need this? Is this a priority for us? These are vital "we" questions that many couples try very hard to avoid. Let's look at these questions more carefully . . .

Can we afford this?
Translation: Is this something we can *both* afford?
Incorrect Translation: This is something *I* can afford, even if it puts financial pressure on *you.*

Do we need this?
Translation: Is this something we *both* need, and *both* should be contributing to?
Incorrect Translation: This is something *I* need, and expect *you* to contribute to.

Is this a priority for us?
Translation: Is this something we *both* want to be spending money on right now?
Incorrect Translation: This is something *I* want right now, and expect you to go along with.

The only good answers to these questions are answers that work for *both* partners. But they are critical questions that give each person a chance to express and deal with financial realities in an upfront and healthy way. Otherwise, strange and unhealthy financial arrangements become part and parcel of the relationship.

Money Always Talks—
Make It Talk in the "We"

Are you ready to start asking more questions about money? Are you ready to give up full autonomy and concede that money, regardless of who is earning what and who is spending what, is a couples' issue which, if left unchecked, leads to big-time couples' conflict? Perhaps one of the hardest sentences for two members of a couple to utter is,

"We can't afford this right now." It signals the end of the fantasy phase of a relationship where love was *the* issue, and the beginning of the reality phase where love is just *one* issue. But it is a necessary beginning for a fuller experience of partnership.

Not talking about money is *not* a solution. You may think that, in your silence, you have avoided an unpleasant conversation. But the reality is that when it comes to money issues, silence speaks volumes. Silence conveys distrust, silence conveys disinterest, silence conveys disrespect, silence conveys dishonesty. Most of all, silence maintains *separateness*.

If you have been avoiding dealing with money, it helps to start small. Have small money conversations, ask more small money questions, volunteer more financial information, devise a more balanced solution to everyday bill-paying, create a small, joint cash till. Your goal is to open the door. Creating more of a sense of financial connectedness is a thread-by-thread process. The important thing is that you *start*.

BRINGING STEPCHILDREN INTO THE "WE"

Many of us grew up watching *The Brady Bunch*, a sitcom about a mother of three girls who marries a father of three boys. It goes without saying that there was some adjusting that needed to be done, but with amazing ease both Mr. and Mrs. Brady were able to be great stepparents as well as parents. Faster than you can say "Nick-at-Night," the two households combined to become one big happy family. It seemed so easy on television, but in real life, living with stepchildren requires real maturity and a lot of work.

Recently I had dinner with Maggie and David, old friends who have been happily married to each other for more than twenty years. They were talking about Maggie's son, Danny, who was about to get married himself. Danny was about five years old when Maggie and David met, and back then, he was a real handful. During dinner David was telling me how difficult he initially found it to be Danny's stepfather. He was in love with Maggie, and he saw Danny as little more than an intrusion.

Now David says that one of the things in life about which he feels most proud is his relationship with his stepson. He says that it was Maggie who didn't let him get away with being a perfunctory step-dad. "She was very clear," he told me, "that she wanted her son to be part of our relationship."

When a child is involved, both the natural parent and the new step-parent need to work to be emotionally aware enough to make certain that the child doesn't feel excluded from the new relationship. Once again, you can start creating a sense of family with "we" language and "we" activities.

For example . . .

- Instead of saying, "What would you like for dinner?" try say-ing "What do you think we should have for dinner?"
- Instead of saying, "Would you like to see a movie?" try saying "I think it would be fun if we all went to see a movie."
- Instead of saying, "You and your friends are making us crazy with the loud music," try saying "I think we should sit down and figure out a schedule so that we have some quiet time in the house."
- Instead of saying, "Your mother/father is still asleep; you should eat some breakfast," try saying "Your mother/father is still asleep; why don't we let him/her stay in bed while we make (or go out) for some breakfast."

Making "we" a priority means making EVERYONE feel included.

BUILDING A FUTURE IN THE "WE"

You can plan and plan and plan how your future as a couple will have a stronger experience of "we." You can talk about what your life together will look like—where you will live, how many children you will have, where you will take your vacations. And you can fantasize about what that future will feel like. But the only way to get from here to there is by prioritizing "we" *today* and every day from this day forward. "We" doesn't suddenly happen because you have been together for ten years, or twenty years, or fifty years. "We" happens because you have been consciously taking *daily* steps to make it happen. *Here, in a small capsule, are those daily steps . . .*

- *Speak more "we."*
Don't underestimate the power of simple words like "we," "us," "our," and "ours." Make them a part of your daily sentences, ringing in your partner's ears and in your own ears, working their magic.

- *Act more "we."*
Even the simplest inclusive gestures—a hug, a touch, holding hands—create feelings of love, acceptance, and trust. Don't treat your bond like a secret; pay attention to special gestures and statements that tell the world, "We're a couple."

- *Think more in the "we."*
Even when you are talking to yourself, you should be using "we" language. Don't keep yourself in isolation in your own mind with "I" words. You need to always be reminding yourself that you have a partner, especially when your partner is not close by.

- *Make more "we" decisions.*
Incorporate your partner into your daily decision-making process

and problem-solving process wherever possible. Remind yourself that the majority of your daily decisions affect you *and* your partner. Resist the well-programmed instinct to handle everything by yourself.

- *Allow yourself to feel more "we."*

Explore your resistance to feeling more "we." Don't deflect or minimize your partner's "we" language and "we" actions. Allow yourself to feel the bonding strength of your own "we" behavior. "We" feeling translates into more "we" language and more "we" action which, in turn, reinforces and expands a genuine feeling of "we."

SECRET #4:

Fight Stereotypes

· ◆ ·

When we are lucky enough to find ourselves in a loving relationship, it always feels special and unique. Even so, it's easy to undermine this specialness with behavior that is scripted and stereotyped. Powerful models for relationship behavior and interaction surround us. Our parents taught us—through their words and actions—what a relationship should look like. So did our grandparents, aunts and uncles, siblings, neighbors, and friends. Even if we didn't respect these relationships, they became a part of who we are and preprogrammed us for the future.

Every day we are looking at somebody else's idea of what a relationship should be. We can't avoid it. Our favorite television programs give us images of couples living together—from Lucy and Desi to Dharma and Greg. Our favorite books, magazines, and movies tell us what love should look like. Although we know it's fiction, these messages become part of who we are. Even those of us who are trying very hard to "be ourselves" and establish our own identities know the feeling of acting out somebody else's script.

By the time we're ready to make the transition from being separate to being partnered, we have assimilated hundreds, if not thousands, of other people's scripts. We have learned how you are "supposed to" talk to a partner, how you are "supposed to" act with a partner, how you are "supposed to" argue with a partner, how and when you are "supposed to" have sex, and how you are "supposed to" set up house. We have learned how you are "supposed to" express affection, appreciation, dissatisfaction, love, desire, wants, needs, anger, and fury. Combine all this with the scripts and stereotypes from our own experiences in romantic relationships, starting with our very first crush. That's more scripts than even the most powerful Hollywood studios have.

But relationship scripts, however compelling, do not acknowledge either the unique individuality of each member of the couple or the unique personality of the couple itself. Whenever we follow a script and try to do it by the book, we move further and further away from a balanced, loving partnership and closer to a caricature that is fragile, stagnant, and superficial—as well as self-defeating. Even if our relationship *looks* connected, scripts and stereotypes keep us *feeling* very single and separate.

FOUR COUPLES, FOUR STRUGGLES WITH STEREOTYPE

◆ *Gwen and Joshua enjoy going out to dinner often. But whenever they stay home, Gwen finds herself cooking. Gwen used to love making dinner but now she hates it because she can't escape it, and every day she feels a little more resentful. Yes, she is the better cook. And yes, Joshua will help wash the dishes. But why does she have to be in charge? Gwen asks herself this all the time.*

◆ *Although Frank and Darla go to the movies almost every weekend, Frank assumes full responsibility for the activity. Frank has to get the newspaper; Frank has to find out what's playing; Frank has to figure out the time schedule. And then Frank presents this to Darla. Every week that Darla remains a passive participant, Frank feels a little more annoyed. Frank asks himself, "Why do I have to work so hard to do something that's supposed to be relaxing?"*

♦ *Alexis and Martin are arguing because Alexis is convinced that if she didn't assume total responsibility for picking up their three-year-old son Eddie from day care, he would never get home. Martin loves his son, but he says he doesn't have the time. Alexis is just as busy as Martin, but she has to find the time, and this makes her angry. Alexis thinks to herself, "Martin is a bigger child than Eddie."*

♦ *Bonnie and Ezra have been together for three years. But whenever they go out, Bonnie still expects Ezra to pay for everything. Bonnie wants Ezra to "be the man" and take her out. But Ezra is stewing over Bonnie's expectations. His way of responding is to silently "punish" Bonnie by not going out at all. Ezra thinks to himself, "Bonnie earns lots of money, and our relationship has passed its 'just dating' phase—why can't she share expenses sometimes?"*

Pour Behavior into a Mold and Watch It Harden into a Problem

These four couples are engaged in classic relationship struggles. They are not fighting over fidelity, or integrity, or the absence of love. But they *are* fighting, though the arguments are typically silent.

All of these couples have poured certain aspects of their relationship into a mold, and let it harden into a problem. They have bought into a relationship script that is telling them how they *must* behave.

Certain "musts" are crucial in a relationship. There must be fidelity. There must be commitment. There must be honesty. There must be fairness. These are non-negotiables. But then there are the "musts" that ignore our individuality, throw the relationship out of balance, and stand in the way of growth.

"Why am I always the one who has to do the shopping?" "Why am

I the one who has to work the barbecue?" "Why am I the one who has to initiate sex?" "Why am I the one who has to drive the cheaper car?" "Why am I the one who has to keep track of the bills?" "Why am I the one who has to pack the bags when we go on vacation?" "Why am I the one who has to clean the litter box, or wake up when the baby cries?" "Why am I the one who has to assume responsibility for checking the locks and turning off the lights every night?" "Why am I the one who has to wash the bathroom floor?" Every day that we have to ask ourselves questions like this we are experiencing a sense of separation and distance from the person we want to love *more*.

Hard and fast relationship rules and roles are convenient because they don't ask us to think, or feel, or challenge, or grow. And there's a sense of comfort when the world is well-defined. But hard and fast relationship rules and roles are also self-defeating if your goal is a loving, enduring partnership. For both individuals to flourish in a relationship, and for a couple's unique "personality" to emerge, every unhealthy rule must be questioned, and every limiting role must be challenged. Consider the following list.

Popular Relationship Stereotypes

- Women are more in touch with their feelings; men don't know how to nurture.
- Men are better at handling bill-paying and finances.
- Women settle into long-term relationships primarily for security; men settle into long-term relationships primarily for sex.
- Men are naturally messy.
- Women, no matter how smart or successful, are expected to take on more household responsibilities.
- The man should be in charge of making the important decisions.
- Women are the intuitive sex.
- In the kitchen, the woman is the boss.
- Men and women are from different planets.

Even if we know in our heads that these things are not true—even if we *know* that every individual is unique, and that the emotional, sexual, financial, and day-to-day organization of every couple should be unique—we still cave in around these stereotypes.

GETTING CLEAR ABOUT STEREOTYPES

How do you start to fight these stereotypes? It helps a lot to be clear, in your mind and heart, that . . .

- Not a single one is ever true or accurate for *all* men or *all* women—many are completely distorted, convoluted, or false, and . . .
- *Every* single one is potentially destructive if it gets between you and your partner.

When you are invested in stereotypes, believing in broad generalizations and using labels and language that depersonalize your partner and your relationship, you stop seeing your partner as a person. This creates distance and separateness. Building a loving partnership means creating a bond that is unique. You will never create that bond successfully if you are constantly slashing at your relationship with the broad sword of stereotype.

When partnership is your goal, you can *never* put your partner in any category that starts with the words "All men are . . . ," "All women are . . . ," "All men want . . . ," or "All women want. . . ." You have to rid your vocabulary of phrases like, "Because he's a man!" or "Because she's a woman!" or "That's so typical!" If you're going to start describing your partner, describe him/her as an *individual*. Whether your sentiments are negative or positive—and it's okay if some of them are negative—let them reflect who your partner is as an *individual*.

Personalize Your Criticism and Your Praise

Whether you are talking about the most positive or most negative traits, the quirkiest or most stereotypical traits, use your partner's name to break the negative barrier of stereotype. For example . . .

- Can you see the difference between saying (or thinking), "Fred has a hard time expressing his anger," and "Men can't express their emotions"? One reflects who Fred is and what his personal emotional struggle is; the other tells us nothing.
- Can you see the difference between saying (or thinking), "Janet's feelings get hurt very easily," and "Women are so emotional"? One gives us a picture of Janet, the human being who is vulnerable; the other trivializes her feelings.
- Can you see the difference between saying (or thinking), "Joseph has never made cleaning the house a priority," and "All men are messy"? One gives us a picture of Joseph's personal priorities; the other dismisses all men as hopeless.
- Can you see the difference between saying (or thinking), "No one ever showed Desra how to balance her checkbook," and, "Women aren't any good with bill-paying and finances"? One gives us a clear picture of Desra's lack of experience with specific financial issues; the other dismisses all women as helpless.

Notice, in the following examples, how a person's nature, special talents, or gifts can be highlighted by focusing on the individual, or diminished and dismissed with stereotypical comments or thoughts.

- Can you see the difference between saying (or thinking), "Herbert is such a fine tennis player," and "Men are naturally more athletic"? One gives us a picture of Herbert's special talent; the other actually diminishes that talent by suggesting that all men are the same and just like Herbert.

Fight Stereotypes

- Can you see the difference between saying (or thinking), "Elena has such a loving heart," and "Women are the nurturing sex"? One gives us a clear picture of Elena's warmth and specialness; the other actually ignores that specialness.
- Can you see the difference between saying, "Josephina loves to cook gourmet meals," and "Women are more comfortable in the kitchen"? One gives us a clear picture of Josephina's passion; the other actually dismisses that passion.
- Can you see the difference between saying (or thinking), "Elvin has incredible organizational skills," and "Men are naturally 'left-brained'"? One gives us a clear picture of Elvin's hard working nature; the other actually *dismisses* his hard work.

Take these examples to heart and start thinking of ways to personalize your criticism *and* your praise. In the best of times, the worst of times, and all the times in between, *your partner is an individual*. And you are, too.

Practice Role Reversal

I'm sure that *you* don't want to be lumped into any category. So here's a short assignment. Take some time right here, right now, to think about what it feels like when you are lumped into a category. How do you react when you're on the receiving end of any stereotype? Recall those uncomfortable experiences of feeling invisible, unrecognized, unappreciated, or obliterated by someone else's insensitive label. Recall the feelings of being attacked by accusations like, "You're just like every other woman!" or "You're just like every other man!" Why do that to your partner?

Now take a few more minutes to switch roles, put yourself in your partner's shoes, and give some serious thought to the stereotypes you've been applying to your relationship. Try to imagine what it feels like for your partner to be subjected to these stereotypes. Feel the distance that it creates. Role reversal is a powerful way to experience the weight of our own words and actions.

Recognize That "Typecasting" Isn't Always a Gender Issue

Not every relationship stereotype breaks down along gender lines. Many of the most powerful stereotypes, for example, are those that reenact old parent-child dramas. One partner is always the irresponsible child, the other is the overresponsible father. One is the helpless infant, the other is the controlling mother. But "mother" or "father" are not necessarily female and male: men often find themselves playing the part of mother; women can find themselves cast as the father.

Roles are often created in the first weeks of a new relationship when each partner is revealing their areas of strength. But this can harden into a problem when growth possibilities are shut out. For example, she is "the creative one" and he is "the sensible one." This dismisses *her* creativity, and it doesn't allow *him* to cut loose. Or how about this division of roles: she's the smart one, and he's the plodder. This dismisses his brains, and it dismisses her struggle to achieve. Just because someone has certain talents or strengths, it doesn't mean they should be typecast for the life of the relationship. Once again, this is a surefire path to resentment.

Patterns are also created in the first weeks of a new relationship when each partner is trying hard to be perfect. But these micropatterns often harden into stereotypical behavior patterns that feel inescapable. For example: She always picks the restaurants; he always picks the movies. She always controls the remote; he always controls the lights. She always vacuums; he always empties the dishwasher. This division of labor may work for a while, but ultimately both partners feel shut out because they have too much responsibility in certain circumstances, and no voice at all in others. Then there are the "couples" patterns: Thursday night is always movie night, Friday night is reserved for sex, Sunday is always pasta for dinner. These patterns can easily become oppressive if one or both partners feel they must *always* comply.

Liberate Yourself from Your Own Romantic History

Many of our ugliest stereotypes are built and fortified during the years we spend in unsuccessful relationships. Tough emotional times make for tough attitudes, and it's hard sometimes to stay open-hearted, optimistic, and stereotype-free. These are the times when, in spite of our best intentions, we can find ourselves starting to embrace the party line, focusing on the worst traits of the opposite sex and accepting popular relationship rhetoric, including: "All relationships are hopeless."

When a positive, promising, healthier relationship finally appears on the horizon, these stereotypes do not necessarily dissolve. More typically, we push them underground but still keep them as part of our subconscious arsenal. For awhile, we may feel free of these destructive sentiments. But when the positive, promising, healthier relationship road gets a little bumpy—something that happens in *all* relationships, even the most loving ones—it's easy to take those ugly stereotypes out of storage and take aim at our partners. "You're just like all the rest!"

Fighting stereotype often means fighting against the residual anger you carry from your own romantic history. When we don't take on that fight, we run the risk of confusing the present with the past. We treat Fred the same way we treated Ted, Ed, and Jed. We treat Jane the same way we treated Joan, Joanna, and Josephine. And we lose our unique connection.

Fighting stereotype also means reminding yourself that you are starting over in this relationship. Just because it is a loving, healthy relationship doesn't mean it will feel the same or look the same as other positive relationships you have had in the past. You will have different things in common and you will mesh in different ways. The connection will be loving, but different. Your communication will be different. Your behavior will be different. Your rituals will be different. Your pet peeves will be different. The good times will be different; the bad times will be different. The sex will be different. The bond will be special, but different. *No two relationships are ever the same.* If all of your relationships feel the same, something is very wrong.

MORE STEREOTYPES THAT KEEP US DISCONNECTED

Many years ago, when Julia Sokol and I were writing *Men Who Can't Love*, we interviewed a man who was on the verge of leaving his one-year marriage because he felt so trapped by the rigid stereotypes that were controlling the marriage. This man lived with his wife for five years before they got married, and he recalled those years as happy and satisfying. Yet as soon as they got married, everything started to change. Practically overnight, he explained to us, his wife wanted a very different relationship. Marriage, to her, meant the following: As a couple, they should have dinner together every single night, always using the good china. Every Friday they should go out to eat. Every Saturday evening should be spent with another couple. Every Sunday they should be with family, alternating between his family and her family.

For the five years this couple had been living together before they got married, mealtimes were spontaneous and unplanned. Some nights they had dinner together; other nights they didn't. Some nights they ate dinner on their best dishes, some nights they used paper plates, and some nights they ate on napkins while watching TV. And there were no set rules about when they should go out, how often they should go out, or what they should do and who they should do it with. Not surprisingly, this man was feeling suffocated by his wife's new rules.

Playing a Couple vs. Being a Couple

I have met very few people who do not have at least *some* stereotypical notions about what constitutes "appropriate" couple behavior. Here are some of the typical stereotypes that tend to create discomfort, conflict, and sometimes, all-out warfare.

Classic "Couple Behavior" Stereotypes

- "If we're a couple, we share all our money."
- "If we're a couple, we never take separate vacations."
- "If we're a couple, we go to bed at the same time."
- "If we're a couple, we have sex three times a week."
- "If we're a couple, we have two children and a dog."
- "If we're a couple, we put family activities first."
- "If we're a couple, our door is always open to family members."
- "If we're a couple, we should have the same friends."
- "If we're a couple, we do all our socializing together."
- "If we're a couple, we split all expenses fifty-fifty, even if we don't earn the same amount of money."

Turning a loving relationship with great potential into a successful partnership demands integrity, decency, fidelity, respect, and commitment. These are relationship "musts." But most everything else is open to negotiation. *Playing* a couple means playing into stereotypes that are not supportive of who you are and what you need. *Being* a couple means defining yourselves in every area of the relationship—not living with someone else's definitions and feeling frustrated or resentful. Even those men and women who are incredibly well-intentioned can find stereotypical demands repressive and distancing. If you need a rule to live by, try this one:

"To survive and thrive as a couple, we must remain flexible."

HAPPINESS SCRIPTS VS. REAL SCRIPTS

♦ *Zachary has always had a clear picture in his mind of what his life would look like once he met the "woman of his dreams." In the "how we spend our weekends" part of that picture, Zachary envisioned he and his partner taking long drives through the Connecticut countryside looking for antiques and spending the occasional evening at a charming bed-and-breakfast. Then Zachary met Heather, and his happiness script hit a brick wall. Heather manages a store at the local mall and she is required to work Saturdays and Sundays. This leaves no opportunity for long, lazy weekend drives. Zachary is trying to adjust, but he is really struggling. He fears that he and Heather will not make it as a couple if they can't bond during the weekends in the scenario he envisioned.*

♦ *Jesse has also always had a clear picture in her mind of what her life would look like once she met the "man of her dreams." In the "how we spend the weekend" part of her picture, Jesse envisioned herself and her partner doing their grocery shopping together, pinching cantaloupes and planning the week's meals. Then Jesse met Darryl, and her happiness script disintegrated. Darryl detests shopping and can't get out of the supermarket fast enough. He is always willing to take his share of the responsibility for food shopping, but he races through the store like lightning, gets impatient when he can't find things quickly, and complains to the management when the checkout lines are too long. Jesse is finding that she actually feels better when she lets Darryl go to the store by himself, but she is incredibly disappointed that she will never have the experiences she envisioned.*

One of the greatest challenges in a relationship is adjusting to the real, ever-changing scripts of a unique partnership and grieving the loss of fantasy scripts we have held dear. And I do mean truly grieving. When we cling to our fantasy scripts we become critical and judgmental of partners who don't measure up, we become absorbed in fantasies about nonexistent partners who would be more cooperative, and we take one foot out of the relationship we're in.

My earliest experiences in my relationship with Jill were similar to Zachary's experiences. I was most productive working Monday through Friday in an office surrounded by other writers, yet Jill had to work most weekends. After waiting so many years to find a loving partner, I could not get over the fact that we were not going to be living the life *I* envisioned. "Why couldn't we have our weekends together like most *normal* couples?" I would ask myself, clinging to some convoluted fantasy notion of what "normal" (another fantasy) couples do. My disappointment and frustration generated some very real anger, and I held onto this anger for a long time. But finally, it was developing a real-life script that accommodated our real-life circumstances—finding other, more creative opportunities to create the bond that I craved—that put an end to my longing and my anger. Real-life scripts—scripts that are fluid, mutually acceptable, and supportive of real-life demands—are the best antidote to lost relationship fantasies.

RIGID NOTIONS MAKE FOR RIGID EMOTIONS

Last year at a seminar I gave in New York City, a young couple sitting in the front row was eager to air their struggle. The woman had asked her partner to attend the seminar because she was convinced he had a commitment problem. "Last week was my birthday," she began. "He brought home beautiful flowers, took me to a very expensive restaurant for dinner, but didn't get me a present!" she explained. She continued angrily, "I feel this is a mixed message—part of him is holding out on me. Doesn't this sound like commitmentphobia to you?" During this explanation, her partner remained silent.

THIS IS HOW LOVE WORKS

I am always quick to see obvious commitment conflicts. Yet as I looked at this man, I did not see that conflict clearly. What I saw was a person who had failed to fulfill his partner's fantasy birthday script. This man had spent all of his money on flowers and an expensive dinner. Yet this had been completely devalued because it was not the kind of present his partner expected. The gift she needed had to come in a box; even if her partner had spent two weeks' salary on that special dinner, it just wasn't the same. Her partner simply didn't understand this, and now he was suffering the consequences.

Being able to explore the conflicting birthday scripts this man and woman were carrying seemed to provide both members of the couple, and the rest of the audience, with considerable relief. No one was *wrong* here. What this couple needed most was an ongoing exploration of rigid ideas that were keeping them from creating a more loving emotional connection.

I offer this example to you because it is such a good illustration of how we can fail to see what is directly in front of us if it isn't the thing our fantasy tells us we should see. More important, it illustrates this: *We can fail to feel the love in the gifts we are given when those gifts don't come in the package we require.* This woman couldn't feel her partner's love because he didn't act out her script. Her rigid notions created rigid emotions. She was left feeling angry, he was left feeling cold and distant.

Consider some of the rigid notions you may be holding on to that keep *you* from feeling loved and more connected to your partner.

How We Stereotype "Feeling Loved"

- "I don't feel loved if I don't get flowers every week."
- "I don't feel loved if my partner wants to spend time with her/his friends."
- "I don't feel loved if my partner doesn't spend money on me."
- "I don't feel loved if my partner doesn't call me every hour."
- "I don't feel loved if my partner doesn't want to make love to

104

me every day."
- "I don't feel loved if my partner doesn't cook for me."
- "I don't feel loved if we don't like the same things."
- "I don't feel loved if my partner doesn't compliment me constantly."
- "I don't feel loved if my partner won't share *everything* with me."
- "I don't feel loved if my partner discourages my sexual advances."
- "I don't feel loved if my partner won't take me out somewhere fun every weekend."
- "I don't feel loved if my partner doesn't give me his/her complete attention whenever I am talking."

It's time to stop focusing on the negative—time to stop focusing on script deficiencies and start focusing on the unique aspects of your relationship that should be celebrated. How *does* your partner express love? What gifts have you received that you may have minimized or dismissed? Make a list of these things—a "love list"—and keep it in a visible place. Add to it whenever possible. Review this list often, and let it keep you focused on how much love already exists in your relationship. A loving partnership takes hold when both partners are able to start dismantling their rigid notions about love and start paying more attention to the loving gestures that are easy to dismiss or devalue because they aren't part of a script.

WHAT DID YOU LOSE WHEN YOU FOUND YOUR PARTNER?

Angela and Gary have been dating for two years, and living together for the past eight months. Living together has created an unexpected amount of strain on the relationship, and the primary source of that strain is a relationship script that Angela can't relinquish.

Both Angela and Gary work at home in the small two-bedroom house that they share. Angela works at home as a freelance journalist, and Gary is a clarinet teacher. When Gary's younger students come to the house, Angela finds it very difficult to stay focused on her work. She feels responsible for entertaining these children while they're waiting for their lessons, for talking to the parents, and for making sure every child has a ride home. Occasionally Gary asks Angela for this help, but most of the time Angela takes on these responsibilities automatically. She isn't happy about this; it is not what she really wants to be doing. But in Angela's mind, this is what it means to be a good partner. Not surprisingly, other things are going through Angela's mind too . . . like the frequent headaches she has been getting for the last three months.

Angela is paying a terribly high price to fulfill her "good partner" script. She is compromising her work. Even more destructive, she is sacrificing her essential self to "do the right thing" for Gary. And her "self" is telling her loud and clear, through the frequent headaches, that she is not taking good care of Angela.

One of the most painful and destructive sacrifices we can make for our relationship is the sacrifice of our essential self. When we betray our own nature and our own needs to follow some script, we may *think* we are doing the right thing, but what we are really doing is setting the stage for distress and potential disaster. **Part of building a more enduring partnership is to reclaim the essential things we have sacrificed to follow a relationship script.**

Betraying our true self is certainly the biggest loss we endure for the sake of a relationship, yet it is not the only loss. Most of us also have a laundry list of smaller, very specific things we can no longer have, we no longer want, and we no longer do once we are part of a couple. These items, and the non-negotiable losses attached to them, have their roots in the various relationship scripts and rigid notions we have absorbed and accepted into our belief system. Here are just a few examples . . .

Rigid Notions Create Unnecessary Losses

- "I gave up my Wednesday poker game because that's a single-guy thing."
- "I gave up my painting because I didn't want to subject my partner to the mess."
- "I gave up my adult education classes because I thought it would seem too self-involved."
- "I gave up my old sofa that I loved because his was newer."
- "I gave up my favorite pots and pans because it seemed strange to have two sets of cookware."
- "I gave up reading at night because I didn't want the light to bother her."
- "I gave up eating in bed because I didn't want to look like someone who never stopped eating."
- "I gave up my annual seven-day retreat because I didn't think it was right to leave her alone."
- "I gave up my cat because he's not a cat person."

Reclaiming the Losses
(Before the Resentment Is Too Great)

Note the subtle stereotypes and relationship scripts that are woven into many of previous statements. To build a more enduring partnership, it's important to reclaim the smaller things you have lost to scripts and rigid notions. Maybe your partner needs a little space and *wants* you to play poker with your friends once a week. Maybe your partner is inspired by your creativity and *wants* you to paint. Maybe your partner appreciates your sentimental attachment to your old sofa and *wants* you to keep it. Do you see where I'm going here?

Many relationship problems like these are created when we make one-sided decisions about what our partner may or may not want, or can and cannot handle. These decisions are destructive monsters of our own creation. In a loving, effective partnership there is no place for one-sided decisions like these. Instead, decisions must become *mutual* decisions where everything is open to discussion and nothing is carved in stone.

REPLAYING THE OLD FAMILY FOOTAGE

Vikki, the vice-president of a small advertising firm, commutes into Manhattan five days a week from the remote suburbs of Connecticut. That means four hours of driving and train riding every day. She wakes up at 5:30 in the morning and gets home around 8:00 at night. At this point in the evening, she does the very same thing her mother always did: she starts making dinner for her husband. Most nights, Vikki does not want to make dinner, but she feels that is part of her job as a partner.

Vikki's younger sister Carrie is a stay-at-home mom who has taken a vow that she will never live the life that her mother and sister live. Carrie cooks three days a year—Christmas, Thanksgiving, and Easter Sunday. For the rest of the year she relies on her husband, her housekeeper, and take-out menus. Carrie would actually like to cook more often, but she's so afraid of getting trapped in the kitchen like her mother and sister that she feels she has to maintain this defiant stance.

I have been sharing the story of Vikki and Carrie at my *What Smart Women Know* seminars for many years. It's usually a part of my "opening monologue," because I love to hear the reactions in the crowd: the laughs of recognition, the groans, the discomfort, the puzzlement.

Both Vikki and Carrie, in very different ways, are replaying their old family footage. Vikki, on the one hand, has completely succumbed to the old script that she witnessed growing up, and is trying desperately to superimpose that script onto the new-millennium reality of working a full-time job. That's got to hurt. Carrie, on the other hand, is stuck in what I call an *anti-script*. She's sacrificing a source of great pleasure in order to rebel against a script that feels frightening. Ironically, the rigid script of her rebellion has taken away her freedom, too. She's only replaced one powerful script with another. It is more subtle, but it is there. And this can hurt, too.

Whose Rules Are You Living By?

How are *you* controlled by old family footage? What scenes do you feel condemned to repeat? What scenes have you sworn to never repeat? How do these scripts and anti-scripts control your life and keep you from being more open and flexible in your partnership? Most of us have some awareness of the family patterns we repeat, even when we still feel controlled by them. But it is my experience that very few of us have a real awareness of the defensive "anti-scripts" we have created to fend off uncomfortable family history.

When I hear someone emphatically say something like, "I will *never* cook," or "I will *never* buy a house," or "I will *never* live in the suburbs," or "I will *never* have children," or "I will *never* share my money," or "I will *never* wash a dish," or "I will *never* get a real job," or "I will *never* get married," I know that they are still prisoners of old relationship footage. *Part of the process of making yourself more available for a balanced partnership is freeing yourself from the subtle prison of these "nevers."*

In addition to the old family footage, also think about the family *expectations*—both old and new—that are scripting your relationship. How is your relationship behavior a way of trying to please, impress, or compete with your parents, grandparents, and siblings? How might certain behaviors be your way of *defying* their expectations? On the road to a more effective partnership it is very important to constantly ask yourself very simple but potent questions like, *"Why did I do that?" "Why did I say that?" "Why do I put my family's expectations above the unique needs of my partnership?"* and *"Whose relationship is this anyway?"*

SHEDDING THE SKIN OF FAMILY HISTORY AND FAMILY EXPECTATIONS

There is nothing more daunting than the task of freeing ourselves from the invisible grip of unhealthy family history and convoluted family values. And it is *everyone's* struggle. These are the ideas and examples we lived with every single day of our young lives. We were immersed in them. We ingested them. For some of us, they were our *only* reality, and we wear them today like a second skin. Following these old scripts and fulfilling family expectations is one very significant way we stay emotionally bonded to our family and, in a very primitive way, try to ensure that our family will always love us. This is not always a conscious process, and that makes it so very powerful, as well as tricky. Following anti-scripts and angrily defying expectations is another way of staying bonded to our family—bonded to the anger we have collected in that family. But this old, unhealthy bond often stands in the way of the new loving bond you are trying to build with your partner.

Taking Steps Toward Powerful Change

Whether you are repeating family history and fulfilling family expectations, or rebelling against the entire package, you are still struggling with the impact of family scripts. How do you break these chains and free yourself to be more available to your partner, and more available to your true self? This is not a simple process, but it can be accomplished if you are committed to undoing these scripts. *Always keep in mind these three very important things:*

1) Recognizing the power of these scripts and your angry anti-scripts is the first step to creating something new in your relationship today.

2) Challenging that power, by questioning the origins, the wisdom and the value of all these scripts, anti-scripts, and stereotypes is the

second step to creating something new in your relationship today.

3) Challenging *yourself* to undo the counterproductive scripts and angry anti-scripts is the third step to creating something new in your relationship today. This may take time and considerable effort, but it is the most rewarding step.

BEDROOM SCRIPTS:
WHEN SEX KEEPS US SEPARATE

Sexual intimacy has the potential to make us feel blissfully connected to the one we love. But when your sex life is being controlled by a script, sex can lead to frustration, anger, a sense of distance, and a feeling of disconnection.

Ten years ago, conducting research for the book, *What Really Happens In Bed*, I got my first comprehensive picture of the bedroom scripts that create problems in otherwise loving relationships. Many of these scripts start during our single, fantasy-driven days. But they don't always stop when we find a partner. Here are just a few of the typical scripts and stereotypes—the sexual myths and misunderstandings—that men and women regularly mentioned during their interviews . . .

Sexual Myths and Misunderstandings

- "Normal couples have sex at least twice a week."
- "A loving couple should be, sexually speaking, in perfect accord."
- "It's the man's job to initiate sex."
- "A man doesn't need any physical stimulation to get an erection."
- "An absence of orgasm means an absence of desire."
- "Women don't really enjoy sex."
- "A woman's orgasm isn't that important."

- "Men only care about their orgasms."
- "Women like their sex rough."
- "Birth control is the woman's responsibility."
- "Birth control is the man's responsibility."
- "Physical affection always has to lead to sex."
- "The best sex is spontaneous sex."
- "Penetration is always enough to bring a woman to orgasm."
- "If you have a partner, you shouldn't need to masturbate."
- "A woman's job is to please her partner."
- "If a man can't get an erection, it means he doesn't love you."
- "During lovemaking, the woman doesn't belong on top."
- "Premature ejaculation is a sign of a controlling partner."
- "If a man loses his erection, it's his partner's fault."
- "A man should always know what his partner needs."
- "Aging should not affect sexual desire or sexual performance."
- "Oral sex is not really sex."

If you are nodding your head in agreement with any of the items on this list, your bedroom may not be the pleasure palace you think it is.

What You Really Need to Know About Sex and Relationships

When it comes to sex, every single person is different, and every single couple is different. Noticing those differences, talking about those differences, accepting those differences, and adjusting to those differences is the only way to create a loving bridge. This doesn't happen in an afternoon, or in a single evening of perfect passion. Like all of the other scripts and stereotypes we have discussed in this chapter, dismantling sexual scripts and stereotypes is an ongoing process. Much more of the work takes place in your head than it does in your bed.

Make Your Partner Feel Liked

• ◆ •

Respect. Admiration. Appreciation. Acceptance. Approval. Enjoyment. In this chapter, we're going to focus on a simple four-letter word that conveys these very complex relationship essentials, and that word is: *l-i-k-e*. The members of every truly loving, successful couple know how to make their partners feel respected, admired, appreciated, approved of, enjoyed, and accepted. They know how to make their partners feel liked.

IT'S EASY TO LEAVE "LIKE" BEHIND

Does your partner *know* that you are in love? I'm sure your answer is an emphatic "Yes!" "Alex knows I love him . . . I tell him all the time." "Shirley knows I love her . . . she can see it in my eyes." You can probably recite all the ways you express your love—the number of times you say "I love you," the number of times you hug each other and hold each other, the number of times you make love, the number of loving gestures that you always make. But here is a much tougher question, and I want you to think a bit before you answer: Do you make your partner feel *liked*? Really *liked*? Are you certain? How, exactly, do you make this known?

This is not a chapter about love. Love is a given in every successful relationship, and the members of a couple are likely to be very attuned to how and when they express that love. Everyone knows that without an awareness of love, relationships quickly disintegrate. But love is only one piece of the successful relationship equation. Another, equally important piece, is something that is far less obvious, something that is often completely ignored: the "like."

Think about some of the things you do with friends that you really like. You talk. Exchange compliments. You ask for advice. You do things spontaneously. You do something silly. You share confidences. You play. Now think about how many of these things you do *regularly* with your partner. Do you and your partner have a *consistent* experience of real friendship? *In long-term relationships, it is too easy to assume that "the love" is enough, and to leave the "like" behind.*

BEING IN LOVE IS NOT THE SAME AS BEING IN LIKE

Truth is, many couples who are very much in love are *not* always very much in like. How often have we heard: "I love Bill; I just don't like him when he's angry." Or, "I love Jane; I just don't like some of her values."

Many of us have had the experience of being disliked by someone who loved us. Perhaps we had that first experience from a parent who told us, "Of course I love you—I will always love you; I just don't like you right now." Or we had it from a sibling who remarked, "I love you because you are my sister, but I don't like you as a person." Maybe you have had something similar told to you by a previous partner. This is very confusing. And very hurtful. But it also leaves us with the understanding that "love" and "like" are not one and the same. And even if one is forever, the other can change like the wind.

Your partner needs an equally consistent experience of both your love AND your like. Otherwise, regardless of how much you profess your love, you are not really *expressing* that love, and your partner has no reason to *assume* anything. Take a moment right here to ask yourself the following questions. Your honest answers will help you become more aware of how effectively and consistently you are bringing your partner the "like" in your heart.

Do You Know How to Express Your "Like"?

- Do you freely share many negatives but fail to consistently and regularly share positives?
- Do you know how to give your partner the experience of being liked? Think of two good examples you can recall from this week.
- Do you know how to convey your genuine appreciation, approval, respect, admiration, or acceptance in a way that has your partner walking away feeling, "My partner really likes me"?
- Do you know how to "play" and have fun with your partner? When was the last time you played (excluding playful sex)?
- Do you prioritize friendship with your partner the same way you prioritize sex?

These very simple questions tend to stop a lot of very *loving* partners in their tracks. Perhaps they're having the same effect on you right now. That's okay. "Like" is not something *many* of us are very good at expressing clearly and consistently, and I include myself in that "many." This should not suggest that you are a bad partner. It should only suggest that you need to be more conscious of the value of "like."

EXTERNALIZING THE INTERNAL AND LEARNING THE LANGUAGE OF "LIKE"

Every day we interact hundreds of times with our partners. This interaction starts the moment we wake up in the morning, and doesn't end till we have fallen fast asleep at the end of the evening. We interact around the bathroom, around the television, around our pets, and around the toaster. We watch each other dress and undress, make phone calls, take naps, pay bills, and floss. And for every single interaction, we are not dispassionate observers. We watch. We learn from each other. We appreciate. We approve. We get annoyed. We disagree. Sometimes what we see makes us smile; sometimes it makes us frown. Sometimes it makes us lose interest; sometimes it makes us feel even more in love. But something is *always* happening. There are *always* feelings attached.

Yet often we don't articulate those feelings—especially the positive ones. We have thousands of little conversations in our head, but we don't bring that dialogue into the room. *Consider these examples . . .*

- Alan watches Barbara on the phone with her mom and thinks to himself, "It's great the way she always handles her mother's intrusive questions." But typically, he says nothing.
- Bettina watches Frederick making a pizza from scratch and thinks to herself, "He's so playful and creative." But she doesn't tell him this.
- Brandon watches Felicity working out on the treadmill every day and thinks to himself, "She has so much self-discipline it's remarkable." But 95 percent of the time, he says nothing.
- Justine watches Evan at the computer doing his work and often thinks to herself, "He's so smart!" But it doesn't occur to her to communicate her appreciation.

116

In each of these examples—in each of these moments when so much is felt yet nothing is said—an opportunity for expressing "like" is lost.

If You're Thinking It, Try Saying It

Making your partner feel liked is often as easy as taking positive voices that are often completely clear inside of your own head and opening your mouth to bring them into the room. In other words, say it to your partner, instead of keeping it to yourself.

- If, for example, you are thinking, "He looks great in turtleneck sweaters," try saying, "You look great in turtleneck sweaters."
- If, for example, you are thinking, "She's so good at nurturing important friendships," tell her, "I'm so impressed by the way you maintain your friendships."
- If, for example, you are thinking, "His vulnerability is so endearing," tell him, "I'm so touched by your ability to be so open."
- If, for example, you are thinking, "She handled that difficult assignment so well," let her know what you admired.

Learning the language of like means learning to share your praise in a generous, consistent, and ongoing fashion. It means never tiring of saying things like, "That's wonderful," "That's really special," "That's so smart," "That's so beautiful," and the simple but incredibly effective "Wow!"

Nobody needs years and years of therapy to learn to talk this way. The sentences are not complex, and they are already in your brain. This is not tough stuff—yet it is the stuff we regularly fail to do in our relationships, depriving our partners of a consistent experience of our "like" and cheating ourselves out of a stronger connection.

YOUR POSITIVE FEEDBACK STRENGTHENS TIES

Maybe it feels as though communicating your appreciation (*i.e.*, your "like") is stating the obvious. Maybe that's why you don't bother to say anything. Yet whether it is obvious or not, it doesn't really matter. Your partner still needs positive feedback, and needs to hear it as often as you are feeling it. And it needs to be in your words because what is completely clear to you is not always clear to your partner. His or her head may be filled with doubt, questions, fear, negativity, or self-deprecating voices. Your positive voice can make all of the difference, particularly if your reinforcement is consistent.

One of the things I appreciate most about my wife is her natural ability to convey her "like." She never stops telling me about the ways I help her, engage her, impress her, comfort her, or put a smile on her face. Big things and small things seem equally important to her. The way I arrange my work files. The way I carve a turkey. The way I talk to our cats. The way I turn a phrase. If there is something about me she values—even if it is something very small—she is quick to point it out. For me, however, this is not as easy or as natural.

While I have always been able to make my feelings of love clear to my wife, I have not always done that well with the "like." I tend to regularly dismiss my own thoughts and feelings of "like" as being too small to mention, not worth bringing to her attention, not a priority, or already obvious. I tell myself, "She already knows that" or "She wouldn't believe me" or "I told her that just last week" or "I'll say something later." And then the moment passes and the opportunity is lost.

Yet, being consistently on the receiving end of so much "like" from my wife, I am slowly learning that every time I talk myself out of a "like" moment, I am depriving her of what she deserves and I am depriving the relationship of something special. Everyone is cheated when we don't express the "like" that we feel.

MAKING A "LIKE LIST"

One of the very first things I did to help change my behavior with my wife was to actually sit down and make a list of things about her that I really *liked*. Big things and small things, serious things and silly things. I call it my "like list," and to this day I continue to add to the list. It is my reality checklist I can refer to from time to time, and use to evaluate whether or not I have am doing a good job of regularly conveying my "like." Having a list also makes it easier for me to stay more focused on the positive aspects of our relationship, and less caught up in small struggles.

If you suspect that *you* are doing a less than exemplary job of conveying *your* like, I encourage you to make your own "like list." It doesn't have to be gushy, just clear and straightforward. Start with the very basics, such as, "I like my partner's smile" and "I like my partner's sense of humor." No negatives and no caveats—only 100 percent pure *like*. When your list feels fairly complete, ask yourself, "Does my partner know everything I have written on this list?" "Am I sure?" "When was the last time I made each of these things clear?" Use your list as a way to wake yourself up, and as a point of departure for a different style of interaction. Add to your list whenever possible.

SOME SIMPLE GUIDELINES FOR EXPRESSING MORE "LIKE"

When it comes to talking about your feelings of "like" I have also found the following guidelines to be very helpful:

• *Say what's on your mind when it's on your mind.*
When you're having positive thoughts and feelings about your partner, verbalize them "in the moment." Open your mouth and let it out in simple, direct language. When you wait, it's never the same.

- *Don't assume anything.*

You don't know what your partner needs to hear, you only know what you are feeling and thinking. It's your job as a partner to share that information—that's your gift.

- *Don't underestimate the value of your praise.*

Maybe you think your praise isn't that important or powerful. Think again. You have no idea how much weight your words carry. Many times, it is the praise from our partner that matters *most*.

- *Don't be afraid to repeat yourself.*

Just because you've said something positive once, twice, or even ten times, it doesn't mean you've said it enough. Let your partner be the one to tell you that he/she has had enough praise.

IS YOUR PARTNER STILL "THE ENEMY"?

Last Christmas I got involved in an intense relationship discussion at an office party with another married man who happened to be a leader of various men's sensitivity groups and workshops in southern California. This man, who I will call Gerald, was talking at length about the struggles of the many men in his groups.

"It's very hard for men!" Gerald exclaimed.

I had no reason to disagree—I think it's hard for everyone. But then Gerald continued with his thought, and this is where I became uncomfortable.

"Let's face it," he said to me, "no matter how much you love your partner, and no matter how hard you try, they *are* the enemy."

For a very long moment, I was silent.

"They," of course, meant "women." And I know that Gerald expected me to agree. But to let that comment pass unchallenged would have been no more constructive than the comment itself. So after my long moment of silence, I answered Gerald the only way I knew how.

"I have to say to you very honestly that there has never been a single day in my marriage that I have viewed my wife as 'the enemy,'" I responded quietly, and with complete sincerity. "We have certainly had our struggles," I said, "and I'm sure that will continue, as it does for everyone, but my wife is my closest *ally*. That's why we're together."

Now it was Gerald's turn to be silent. It was hard to know *what* he was thinking at the moment, but the conversation quickly dissolved. Later that evening I learned that Gerald and his wife had recently separated. Only then was I able to imagine where my words had landed.

This conversation may not seem terribly significant, yet it was a turning point for me, both personally and professionally, and I try to share this story with others wherever I can. Through this conversation I realized that I was taking something in my relationship with Jill—a cornerstone in that relationship—completely for granted: the "like." I also realized I was projecting something onto other people's relationships, assuming that "the like" was always there if the love was there. But this conversation forced me to realize that even the most evolved men and women can still see the ones they love as "the enemy."

A loving, lasting, effective partnership only happens when your partner is your ally.

The label "the enemy" is a popular one, sometimes used half in jest and sometimes used with a cutting edge. But it is so important for all of us to understand that the feelings behind this label help decide the future of our partnership.

When we see our partner as the opposition, every moment is a battle. We can be madly in love, yet, on some level, we are always at war. If you truly believe that the opposite sex is the enemy, you will never trust or understand your partner. And you will never fully open your heart. If you want to break your "singles" mindset and ensure the future of your relationship, you must start thinking of your partner as your ally. If you can't, it is terribly important that you try to understand why you can't, and commit yourself to undoing that "why."

DO YOU TREAT YOUR PARTNER LIKE A PEER?

José has always felt a lot of love for Corrina, who is five years younger than he is. And, on paper, they seem like a very good pair. But Corrina suffers from the "I'm not worthy" syndrome. Corrina is always putting José on a pedestal, telling him how much smarter he is, how much more successful he is, how much more worldly he is, and so on. In the beginning of the relationship José would protest and demonstrate how inaccurate these comparisons were, though he was also flattered. Over time, however, he has stopped protesting. Corrina's extravagant praise has caused José to devalue her, and has made it increasingly hard for him to experience her as an equal partner.

Dyrithe truly loves Angelo, but she's always finding subtle ways to put him down. Sometimes she corrects his spelling, sometimes she mimics his Italian accent, and sometimes she makes fun of his white collar job. Dyrithe, a professional artist with a roller-coaster of a career, was drawn to Angelo because he's so hard working and his professional life is so stable. Yet instead of expressing her admiration, she always seems to be taking pot shots. Angelo has been worn down by Dyrithe's putdowns, and now regularly finds himself questioning her declarations of love.

These two scenarios illustrate another classic relationship trap that disrupts and sometimes dismantles partnerships: lack of real equality.

What does it mean to be a true equal?

- Being a true equal means that being older doesn't make you any better or any worse.
- Being a true equal means that being more intellectual doesn't make you any better or any worse.

- Being a true equal means that being taller doesn't make you any better or any worse.
- Being a true equal means that earning more money doesn't make you any better or any worse.
- Being a true equal means that having more experience doesn't make you any better or any worse.
- Being a true equal means that having more formal education doesn't make you any better or any worse.
- Being a true equal means that being different doesn't make you any better or any worse.
- Being a true equal means that your gender doesn't make you any better or any worse.
- Being a true equal means that you experience each other as equals.

A True Partnership Only Happens Between Equals

Are you constantly putting yourself down while putting your partner's behavior, character, or special qualities on a pedestal?

If your answer is "yes", ask yourself these questions:

- What do I gain from this?
- What old voices from my history (parents, siblings, peers, etc.) am I echoing today?
- How is my low self-esteem creating self-defeating behavior and a power imbalance?
- Why don't I feel I deserve a partner who is my equal?
- What can I do—starting *today*—to change this?

Are you constantly putting your partner down, while putting your own behavior, character, or special qualities on a pedestal?

If your answer is "yes", ask yourself these questions:

- What do I gain from this?
- What old voices from my history am I echoing today?

- Why do I need to make my partner feel bad to make myself feel good?
- What insecurities and self-doubts of my own am I masking by going on the attack?
- Why am I afraid of having a partner who is an equal?
- What can I do—starting *today*—to change this?

In any relationship there are, of course, going to be times when you find yourself looking up to your partner in admiration, and there will probably be more than a few times when you find yourself looking down. But these experiences should not be the experiences that define your relationship. A relationship flourishes when there is balance in it. And your greatest comfort comes from looking at your partner not up or down, but straight across.

WHEN YOUR PARTNER FEELS INCLUDED, YOUR PARTNER FEELS LIKED

Stacey goes to church every Sunday morning at 8:00 A.M. It is something she has been doing since she was a little girl. She's usually back home before her partner Edward has woken up and had his morning coffee. But last Sunday Stacey did something very different. She didn't race off to church; instead, she actually waited for Edward to wake up and shower, and then asked him if he was interested in going with her to an 11:00 A.M. service. To her surprise and delight, Edward, who has never expressed much interest in going to church, said yes.

Last Sunday, Stacey and Edward both took a step closer in their partnership—not because they went to church together, but because of the *way* they came together. Stacey took one step out of her normal routine and extended an offer; Edward took one step out of his normal routine and accepted that offer. Both partners broke new ground, and both were rewarded with a slightly more meaningful sense of partnership.

This doesn't mean that Stacey and Edward are going to attend church together every single Sunday from this day forward. They may never go to church together again. That is not the issue here. The issue is that both partners sent each other an important message last Sunday. Stacey's message was: "I want you to know that you are welcome to be a part of the things that are important to me. You don't have to do this, and I won't be hurt if you don't, but I want you to know that this door is open to you." Edward's message was: "I appreciate the special effort you made to let me know I'm welcome in your world. This may not be something I want to do on a regular basis, but my way of saying 'thank you' today is to accept your invitation."

It can be hard to feel liked when we are feeling excluded. Maybe we don't want to play tennis every Saturday, but we want to know that it's okay to tag along sometimes and watch the game. Maybe we don't want to spend two hours shopping for clothes in Macy's, but we want to know it's okay to tag along sometimes and have a cup of coffee at the mall.

Growing a partnership means . . .

- Telling your partner "My world is open to you."
- Taking small steps into your partner's world when your partner says, "My world is open to *you*."

LOOKING FOR INVISIBLE BARRIERS

Think about the areas in your life where your partner may still feel unwelcome—areas where you continue to act very *un*partnered or where "living single" actions prevail. Do you keep your partner out of the kitchen? Do you keep your partner out of your closets? Do you keep your partner out of your car? Is your business life something you keep off-limits? Is your spiritual life something you pursue on a strictly solo basis? Is your cultural life something you pursue only with certain other friends? Are your recreational choices solitary choices? Have you ever introduced your partner to the members of . . . your men's group? . . . your meditation group? . . . your bridge group? . . . your study group? Have you ever introduced your partner to the guy who cuts your hair?

Try to stop yourself from making too many assumptions. Don't get shut down by thoughts like, "She doesn't have time," or "He wouldn't be interested," or "She'd think it's dumb," or "He wouldn't feel comfortable." Give your partner the chance to have his or her own response. That's part of the "feeling welcome" process.

This is not about control. This is not about manipulation. This is not about losing your healthy independence. And this is not about recreating your partner to be more like you. This is about opening doors. As you struggle to open these doors, and struggle to step through your partner's doors, continue to remind yourself how important it is to make your partner feel liked.

SHARING YOUR PROCESS, SHARING YOUR CHALLENGES

Amy and Clinton have just had a very big argument, and the organizing theme was "not feeling liked." In three months Amy's daughter from her previous marriage is graduating from high school. Amy is trying to organize a party, and is overwhelmed by the many details. Yet Amy has not discussed this struggle at all with Clinton. Amy has assumed, from the very beginning, that this party is something she's going to have to organize herself from start to finish. She certainly doesn't want any help from her ex-husband, and she feels it wouldn't be fair to burden Clinton, who she's been with for only one year. So she's wrestled with all the details quietly by herself, and all Clinton sees is an Amy who is distant and overwhelmed.

Today, Clinton finally asked her to please tell him why she is acting so distant. Amy then blurted out a twenty-minute explanation of everything she's been trying to handle by herself for her daughter's party—the politics (who gets invited from her ex's side of the family), the travel arrangements for Amy's parents, the choice of locations, the food requirements, the options for entertainment, getting a special cake, the works. Listening to this, presented all at once, Clinton got upset. Why hasn't Amy been talking to him about this all along? Why hasn't she asked for his opinions and suggestions from time to time? Yes, he's only known Amy for a year, but why hasn't she given him the option of being more involved? "How can we develop our relationship," Clinton asked angrily, "if you won't include me in your process?"

In spite of Amy's regular declarations of how much she is in love with Clinton, right now Clinton is not feeling liked.

Kenneth and Courtney have also been together for about a year, but Kenneth seems to have a better ability to make Courtney feel liked. Here is just one example of how that reveals itself in their day-to-day relationship. One Sunday of every month, Kenneth takes his mother out to lunch at her favorite restaurant on the New Jersey shore. Courtney sees Kenneth's mother on a number of other occasions, but this is a mother-son ritual that she doesn't need to participate in. Recently, Kenneth's mother has started to complain of serious back pain, and is experiencing obvious discomfort during their thirty-minute car ride to the restaurant. Kenneth is upset by this, and fearful of things to come. But instead of keeping his concerns to himself, he immediately started discussing this with Courtney. They have talked about his mother's overall health, his mother's doctors, his mother's medicine, and his mother's stoic nature. They have discussed possible alternatives to the long car ride, including creating a once-a-month picnic for his mother at her home with her favorite foods from the restaurant. Courtney has even offered to pick up the food for Kenneth from time to time, and to accompany him on the drive.

Kenneth could have excluded Courtney from all of this and felt justified in doing so. He could have decided that this was his mother, and something *he was going to have to handle by himself. After all, he and Courtney have been dating for less than one year. But his decision to include Courtney in his process has yielded an extraordinary payoff: loving support, and increased feelings of partnership. Maybe this is primarily Kenneth's problem right now, but by giving Courtney a window into his process and keeping her in the loop, he has given her a clear sense of being liked.*

The longer we spend time being single, the better we get at "handling" life's challenges. We develop our own problem-solving process, and we work, or muddle, our way through. When a partner comes along, it's very easy to remain in that "single" state of handling challenges alone. When there's a family problem, we work out the solution alone, in our heads. When there's a job problem, or a money problem, or a health problem, we work out the solution alone, in our heads. Our partners see the results and they see our anxiety and stress, but they get confused and alienated because they aren't seeing, or taking part in our *process.*

Here is the classic relationship conversation that highlights these feelings of separation:

> *Partner A:* "Is everything okay?"
> *Partner B:* "It's okay. I can handle it."
> *Partner A:* "But I *want* to help . . ."
> *Partner B:* "It's really okay. I'm fine."
> *Partner A:* (sighs)

It's enough to make any well-intentioned partner sigh, yet it's a conversation that happens regularly in loving relationships.

If you want to make your partner feel truly liked, keep your partner in the loop.

Think about *your* daily process. Think about the challenges you meet without ever consulting your partner or walking him/her with you through the steps. Now put yourself in your partner's shoes and try to imagine what it feels like to not be included. Imagine what it is like to see you stressed, strained, grumpy, or weird without being able to see *why*. For contrast, now imagine what it feels like to be more included—to feel that your partner likes your input, your point of view, the way you think, or just likes to know you're there. Isn't the difference clear?

Maybe you believe that you are doing your partner a *favor* by keeping him or her out of your process. Maybe you believe that you're doing the appropriate thing, or the most efficient thing. But what you are really doing is making it very hard for your partner to feel liked.

Two simple rules of thumb for making your partner feel liked . . .

1) *Ask for help, even if you don't think you need it.* This is not about what *you* need, this is about what your partnership needs: more feelings of inclusion.

2) *Ask for input, even if you're certain you know what that input will be.* You are not a mind reader. Give your partner the chance to surprise you with his or her own unique contribution.

LEARNING THE LESSONS OF ACCEPTANCE

Gwen and Leonard, who are both in their mid-seventies, have been married for over forty years. The strength of their love and partnership is obvious. Sometimes being around them is like being around two newlyweds—they have a sense of enthusiasm and optimism that is rare, and enviable. Gwen says, with a powerful sense of conviction, that acceptance has been the major lesson of her marriage. And Leonard agrees. Thirty years ago, after a particularly foolish argument about "whether or not to wash the car" escalated into a major fight, Gwen and Leonard reached an understanding. They decided that whenever either one of them started feeling annoyed by the other's quirks or differences, he or she would stop and think about how important the relationship was before saying or doing anything. Their primary goal became this: *being more accepting of each other's foibles*.

Every single one of us wants to be accepted for who we are. We want our unique personality, our unique opinions, our unique experience, our unique appearance, our unique world view, our unique struggle, and even all of our unique quirks and weirdness to get the stamp of approval from our partner. Maybe we can't expect our partner to love and embrace all of these things at every single moment, but we need acceptance. It's how we know that our partner genuinely cares. It's how we know we are loved. And it's how we know we are *liked*.

I have never met a man or a woman who didn't have a hard time with some of the differences that come up in a relationship. How can he eat red meat? How can she spend so much time on the phone? How can he give so much money to charities? How can she drive such an old car? How can he wear the same shirt over and over again? How can she be so nice to strangers? How can he like such childish movies? How can she watch so much TV? This kind of stuff comes up constantly. And it can be frustrating sometimes to have a partner who doesn't share your tastes, your opinions, your priorities, etc. But that's the nature of partnership.

Your partner is not perfect, and your partner will never be exactly like you. This I can promise you. And it will never change. So what are you going to do about it? There are two approaches to working with this reality. You can be judgmental, disapproving, and try in vain to control your partner's universe. Or you can learn to accept these imperfections and differences as a part of life, and learn to appreciate them because they are an important expression of your partner's individuality. Only one of these two approaches will ever make your partner feel liked.

ROR

ARE WE HAVING FUN YET?
TIME FOR PLAY, TIME FOR "LIKE"

Sometimes, as we make the transition from being single to being part of a couple, we get so serious—so burdened by the complex emotional content of our relationship—that we completely lose that simple sense of having fun. We lose that ability to hang out and play with our partners, as we do with good friends even as adults. Do you remember that childhood song, "Playmate, come out and play with me . . ."? We "play" with people we *like*, don't we? When was the last time you played with your romantic partner?

♦ *Amber and Benjamin spend at least one Saturday afternoon a month test driving new cars just for fun.*

♦ *Jo and Ellis have already had three pillow fights this year, and it's only the middle of March.*

♦ *Frida and Alex love to go for drives in the summertime looking for local carnivals and street fairs. Every summer they collect dozens of goofy prizes playing "fill the balloon with water" contests.*

♦ *Marta and Billy turn every holiday into an event. They have, for example, just spent three weeks working on their Halloween costumes, and on Halloween night they will be the only two people in their neighborhood over the age of thirty who are going trick-or-treating without any children.*

♦ *Alana and Norman love to surprise each other, and their close mutual friends, with elaborate practical jokes.*

♦ *Georgia and Max still make sandcastles together every time they take a trip to the beach.*

These are couples who know how to play. Whether they realize it or not, their interest in playing with each other conveys strong mutual feelings of "like" and fortifies their bond.

Wise couples make room in their relationship for play, and they regularly make play a priority.

We all know that being a couple is hard work; we also know that life is often challenging. But if you can't remember the last time you and your partner had some fun together—just plain old fun—then you are long overdue.

Play is not just for children. Play is how we express our creativity, how we pay attention to the child in us all, how we connect to pure feelings of joy, and how we lighten our hearts. To play with a partner is to share all of this, and to do it in a way that says "I like who you are, and I like being with you." I'm not talking about elaborate play where it costs thousands of dollars just to have a little "fun." And I'm not talking about competitive play where one partner is having fun at the other partner's expense. I'm talking about good old-fashioned, put-a-smile-on-your-face play.

It doesn't matter if you're out at the movies together or barefoot in the park. It doesn't matter if you're playing soccer or Twister. It doesn't matter if you're laughing out loud or just smiling and feeling happy. All that matters is your willingness to take time as a couple for play. It's an indispensable ingredient in the day-to-day recipe that yields the delicious feeling of being liked.

SECRET #6:

Create
Safe Spaces

• ◆ •

I have read several published studies that say that the blood pressure and pulse rates of men and women in happy and contented partnerships can actually go down when they are together. This tells me that couples living in supportive environments feel *safe* with one another.

On the other hand, when two people are living together in a negative, emotionally hostile environment—be it openly hostile or covertly hostile—one or both of them often complain of a host of unpleasant physical symptoms including headaches, backaches, and digestive distress. This tells me that when people feel threatened—when they can't let their emotional guard down—this absence of emotional safety translates into physical symptoms.

We know, of course, that relationships that are openly abusive don't feel safe. This is true of physical abuse, and it is also true of emotional abuse. It is part of the definition of abuse. It goes without saying that most of us don't want to do anything that is abusive to the one we love. We don't ever want to see ourselves as being abusive. That's the kind of stuff you watch on the six o'clock news, right? Yet there are all kinds of things that one person in a relationship can say or do to make a potentially loving environment feel hostile and unsafe.

DOES YOUR POWER PUT YOUR PARTNER ON EDGE?

We all know what it feels like to be with someone you love and care about. When you love someone, you give that person "power" in your life. You care about what that person thinks and feels about you. Any judgments the person you love makes are very important. Sometimes we become so sensitive to what the person we love is thinking that we respond to the slightest criticism, the smallest gesture, the tiniest change in mood. The people we love can use words, gestures, and tone of voice to make us feel that it's unsafe to take risks. They can make us feel that it's unsafe to argue, unsafe to show vulnerabilities, and unsafe to relax.

For example:

♦ *David complains that Lauren is very "uneven." When he returns home from work every day, he is never certain whether the woman he greets is going to be all hugs and kisses or all frowns and tears. When Lauren is happy, everything is wonderful, but when Lauren is upset, she demands his total attention. David says that Lauren's moods are seriously upsetting his life, and he's reaching the point where he dreads going home at the end of the day.*

♦ *Margo says that whenever she and her husband have an argument about anything, he immediately begins to question the wisdom of the whole relationship. If they can't get along on something as minor as choosing a movie, he reasons, maybe they shouldn't be together at all. Margo is tired of being manipulated and threatened by her husband's ongoing "doubts."*

◆ *Richard says that sometimes his sweet and kind wife gets so angry that she pulls the shades off the windows. This has happened several times in the middle of the night when noisy neighbors have interrupted their sleep. His wife's wild anger may be directed at the neighbors, but it scares Richard.*

◆ *Justin is quite funny, but he also has a mean streak that is very wounding to his girlfriend Ronnie. When Justin is angry, he snipes. He takes potshots at Ronnie's friends, Ronnie's parents, Ronnie's work, and Ronnie's aspirations. Justin does this in what he would consider a "humorous"way, but the humor is mean-spirited. Not surprisingly, living with a sniper has made Ronnie reluctant to open her world to Justin. She doesn't want to give him any new material for his "mean routine."*

These four scenarios illustrate four very different ways that one person can make the relationship unsafe for the other. Lauren's moodiness and unpredictability prevents David from enjoying his return home. Margo's husband's way of catastrophizing every little disagreement has Margo anticipating a breakup. Richard's wife has Richard wondering about his physical safety, and the safety of their children. Ronnie wishes she could wear a sniper-proof vest because it hurts so much to remain in Justin's line of fire.

And while I am sure that the men and women who are acting out their fears, insecurities, anger, or emotional mood swings all consider themselves well-intentioned partners, their behavior is, in my opinion, abusive. In all four of these scenarios there is at least one element that puts the relationship "on edge." And as long as that relationship remains on that edge, hearts are in danger.

If your priority is building a partnership that can flourish, you have to learn to create safe spaces—places where you can be vulnerable and honest, places where you can take risks, places where you can argue without fear and open your heart. And while this is something that *both* partners must be able to create, the very best you can do is lead by example.

ARE YOU SO FOCUSED ON WHAT YOU ARE GIVING THAT YOU DON'T SEE WHAT YOU ARE TAKING AWAY?

Nobody does partnership perfectly. Not even the "experts." Yet it's difficult for every one of us to think about what we might be doing less-than-perfectly, particularly if one of our "imperfections" is that we are doing things that make the relationship unsafe. It is, after all, much easier to focus on what you *give* to a relationship than on what you might be taking away. And it's also much easier to focus on your partner's shortcomings than it is to focus on your own.

To make progress in your partnership, you're going to have to take out that mirror from time to time and scrutinize your behavior. And this is one of those times. It is my experience that almost every man and woman makes mistakes in the safe spaces department, and that mirror will help you identify yours. I am not saying this to make you defensive; I am saying this to prepare you for the slight feelings of discomfort that might be provoked by some of the stories in this chapter. Some of these stories still make *me* uncomfortable. We are all works in progress.

When I start to think about the concept of creating safe spaces in a relationship, I immediately think about one very special woman I interviewed almost fifteen years ago. This woman, whose name was Lee, had recently lost her husband after thirty-one years of marriage. What she said about him has stayed with me for all these years. She said, with complete sincerity, "He never gave me a bad moment."

Now, I know too much about relationships to believe that Lee and her husband had thirty-one years of perfect days. I'm sure they wrestled with many issues, and lived through frustrations, disappointments, and the occasional argument. But what Lee was really telling me was that through all of the years and all the ups and downs, she had never felt *unsafe.* That feeling of complete safety is something we can all create and one we all deserve in our relationships. So let's get to work.

MAKING IT SAFE TO BE VULNERABLE

Adina is standing in front of the mirror staring at herself as she pokes and pinches her nose. Adina's partner Gary walks into the bedroom and sees what she is doing. He has witnessed this before, and he knows the question she is about to ask: "Gary . . . do you think I need to get my nose fixed?" Gary has a lot of options here. He could dismiss her question with a joke, he could be snide, he could show his exasperation because he's heard this question so many times before, he could be mean, he could ignore the question entirely. But if Gary's goal is a closer partnership, he needs to prioritize creating a safety net for Adina. And that means passing up the opportunity to make a joke or a dig, overcoming any urges to dismiss her concerns, and giving Adina his most direct and reassuring answer: "I like your nose exactly the way it is." If this is how Gary feels, this is how he must respond. To do anything else would be taking advantage of Adina's vulnerability and establishing that he is not safe. His response must convey the crucial message, "It's safe to feel insecure around me."

As the example of Adina and Gary illustrates, every time our partner shares a moment of weakness with us, we are in the "land of opportunity." We have an opportunity to advance our own agenda, assert our power, act out our anger, or, in some other way, take advantage of our partner's vulnerability. But we also have an opportunity to build trust. That trust is built when we recognize our partner's vulnerability, and respond in a way that says, "It is safe to feel this way with me."

Think about the many moments in your relationship when your partner lets down his or her guard and exposes a soft spot. Perhaps it is when he is scrutinizing his bald spot in the mirror and looking forlorn. Perhaps it is when she has just removed her makeup and is feeling less-than-glamorous. Perhaps it is when he's just finished a painful telephone conversation with his ex. Perhaps it's when she is watching a sad movie and tears start streaming down from her eyes. These moments happen constantly in a relationship, but they happen less and less if we are not willing to make these spaces safe.

Safe Or Unsafe:
There Is Always a Choice

Here are some more examples of how we are constantly presented with opportunities to make our partner feel more safe or less safe in the relationship:

◆ *Sabre has just asked her partner, "Do you really think I'm pretty?" Sabre's partner could use this as an opportunity to make her insecure ("What do you think?"), jealous ("As pretty as Belinda?"), angry ("That's so superficial!"), and so on. But he could also make her feel loved, appreciated, and safe with some simple, agenda-free reassurance, such as: "You're beautiful."*

◆ *Chaz has just said to his wife, "Sometimes I can't believe that you married me." Chaz's wife could use this as an opportunity to make him insecure ("Sometimes I can't believe it either!"), paranoid ("You're lucky George was already taken."), angry ("You're so insecure!"), and so on. But she could also make him feel loved, appreciated, and safe with some direct, agenda-free reassurance, such as: "I consider myself very lucky."*

◆ *Joseph is sick in bed with a horrible flu that has lingered for weeks. He has just said to his partner, "Being this sick makes me think about what a burden I might be to you when I get old." Joseph's partner could take this moment as an opportunity to scare him ("You're not planning on getting that old, are you?"), dismiss his fears ("Don't be such a gloomy Gus."), make him feel bad ("Just don't get me sick!"), criticize him ("You wouldn't be sick if you took more vitamins!"), and so on. But she could also make him feel cared for and safe with some well-intentioned reassurance, such as: "We have our whole lives in front of us . . . please just focus on getting well."*

◆ *Joyce has just come back from her very first appointment with a psychotherapist, and she is still in tears from the catharsis she experienced. Joyce has just told her husband: "I don't remember crying this much since I was a little kid." Joyce's husband could take this moment as an opportunity to make himself feel superior ("I hope I never have to go to a therapist."), to make her feel worse ("With your family history, it's a miracle you haven't gone through this sooner."), to discount her pain ("You're too sensitive!"), to confuse her ("Are you sure this therapy thing is a good idea?"), and so on. But he could also make her feel understood, accepted, loved, and safe with some straightforward words of support, such as: "This must be really hard."*

When your partner risks being vulnerable in your presence, you can feel very powerful. This quickly becomes a real test of your desire for partnership. Here's the million-dollar question: What will you do with that power? Do you go for the joke because you don't want to feel vulnerable, too? Do you take a swing because it's so easy? Do you insert a little dagger in the soft spot that has just been revealed? Do you use it as an opportunity to assert superiority? Do you use it as an opportunity to settle an old score? Do you seize that power because it feels good? All of these are certainly options, but none of them are constructive partnership options. There is only one *constructive* option: ***When partnership is the priority, your goal must always be to rebalance the power.*** And the only way to accomplish that is to make your partner feel safe.

WHAT'S SO FUNNY ABOUT BEING MEAN?

Sonny makes his living writing humor. Unfortunately, he tends to use his sense of humor inappropriately when it comes to handling his partner Sada's vulnerability. When Sada is feeling insecure, Sonny makes a joke. When Sada is upset and needs to talk about it, Sonny makes a joke. When Sada is feeling a little jealous, Sonny makes a joke. Sonny may look like he's enjoying this, but there is absolutely nothing funny about the way Sonny responds to Sada's vulnerability.

When Sada tries to express this to Sonny, he always responds, "I can't control my funny bone; it's who I am." But Sonny's funny bone is not his real problem. His real problem is that he grew up in a household where everyone had a very hard time showing their vulnerability, so they hid their feelings behind tough words and quick wit. This became their style of communication. But that style left everyone in the family feeling unsafe to express real feelings, and today, that is how Sada feels when she is with Sonny because he is unable to make her feel safe.

Humor is a tricky thing. It can add so much to a relationship if it is appropriate and kind-spirited. Or it can be a dangerous weapon. Even if you make your living writing comedy, like Sonny, there are times when it is *not* okay to be funny. *Here are a few other things we all need to understand about safety and vulnerability:*

- Being funny is nothing to laugh at if you're doing it at your partner's expense.
- Provoking jealousy to control your partner's heart, even if you're doing it "humorously," is cruel and unusual punishment.
- Taking advantage of someone's moments of weakness will never help you build your own strength.
- It takes more courage to be vulnerable than it does to be "tough."
- No one can open their heart until they feel safe.

MAKING IT SAFE TO BE DIFFERENT

◆ *Ashley and Billy are wandering around their local bookstore on a Saturday afternoon. They have just met up at the checkout line. Billy takes one look at the book Ashley is buying and says, "That's such trash."*

◆ *Gerald and Ronni are at the supermarket picking up a few household items. Gerald takes two one-quart containers of orange juice and puts them in the grocery cart. Ronni says, "That's so dumb!" and replaces them with a half-gallon jug.*

◆ *Bert and Nonni are in Chinatown doing a little Christmas shopping. Bert stops at a street vendor and buys a snack. Nonni says, with a holier-than-thou tone of voice, "I can't believe you're going to eat that."*

These are typical exchanges that most couples have. But the problem is that these exchanges are not *clean*. In each of these scenarios, one member of the couple is responding to a difference in taste, style, opinion, or behavior with a harsh judgment. Normal differences have been interpreted as unacceptable or threatening, and a swift, defensive response has been delivered—a response that some would call verbal abuse.

As I mentioned briefly in the previous chapter, it can be difficult to accept differences in a relationship. But when those differences make us insecure or uncomfortable, it's very easy to attack them the way white blood cells attack a foreign object in the body. There's nothing wrong with Ashley's choice of reading material—it's just *different* from what Billy would choose. There's nothing wrong with Gerald's preference for smaller containers—it's just *different* from what Ronni would choose. There's nothing wrong with Bert's taste in food—it's just *different* than Nonni's. But in each instance, one partner had to make the other feel bad or wrong or weird. And their harsh, snap judgments have sent a powerful message: "It isn't safe to be different from me; it isn't safe to be yourself around me."

It's hard for someone to feel loving and close when he or she is also feeling picked on, criticized, or judged. If you have little or no tolerance for differences, and find yourself going on the attack, ask yourself these questions: Why do these differences make me so angry, so frustrated, or so insecure? What fears might be lurking beneath my harsh responses? What am I trying to control? Why can't I be more accepting?

Making it safe for differences means . . .

• learning to bite your tongue, not your partner.
• learning more about what makes you tick.
• learning to express approval and appreciation of those differences (and mean it!).
• confronting your control issues.
• learning not so see them as a threat.

MAKING IT SAFE TO HAVE FEELINGS

Do you ever find yourself saying things to your partner such as:

• "I can't believe that upset you."
• "You're such a worry-wart."
• "You have no right to be angry."
• "That shouldn't make you sad, it should make you happy!"
• "Don't cry."
• "Get over it!"

If your answer is yes, you are guilty of a relationship misdemeanor: trying to talk your partner out of his/her feelings. *You and your partner are not always going to be in perfect emotional agreement because you don't have the same emotional construction.* And you are not going to be in perfect emotional agreement because you don't have the same day-to-day experiences. Sometimes you will have the opposite emotional reaction in the exact same circumstances. Sometimes you won't understand what your partner is feeling. Sometimes you will be feeling absolutely wonderful, and completely annoyed that your partner is in a lousy mood. And sometimes you will be ready to swear in court that your partner is completely nuts. But that's *your* business; don't make it your partner's problem.

It's very easy to fall into the trap of judging your partner's feelings because they're not the same as yours. But making it unsafe for your partner to have certain feelings doesn't help make your partnership sound. When you deny, dismiss, or denigrate your partner's emotional reality your behavior is insulting and hurtful, or just plain crazymaking. Maybe you think you're being helpful, maybe this is your way of "jollying" your partner, or maybe this stems from your own discomfort with certain kinds of emotions. But it is counterproductive, and it creates intense, very real feelings of disconnection.

There's another way that you can make it unsafe for your partner to have certain feelings. This happens when you are the partner who has the "exclusive" on those feelings. Perhaps, for example, you are always very depressed, squeezing your partner into the chronic role of "the upbeat one." Perhaps you are always fearful, forcing your partner to be "the confident one." Perhaps you are always anxious, squeezing your partner into the role of "the even-keeled anchor."

Sometimes we get so lost in our own emotional whirlwind that we don't realize how much we are obliterating our partner's feelings. Our terrible sadness trivializes their smaller sadnesses. Our phobias overshadow their smaller fears. Our big joys obliterate their smaller joys. There is no balance. But when partnership is a priority, balance has to be a priority. You have to remind yourself that your partner is entitled to get a little depressed, too. Or fearful. Or anxious. Or angry. Or excited. Or all of the above. And you have to make room for those feelings, and make it clear they are welcome.

Making it safe for feelings means . . .

- understanding how hard it is for "little" feelings to get expressed when larger feelings dominate the relationship landscape.
- not using the weight of your emotions to control your partner's emotions.
- dismantling your emotional landmines.

MAKING IT SAFE TO RELAX AND BE HUMAN

◆ *Ann-Beth won't walk around the house in her underwear because she knows that her husband will ask her if she is gaining weight.*

◆ *Manny has a hard time having a real conversation with his girlfriend Licia because she is always correcting his grammar.*

◆ *Every time Hannah puts dirty dishes in the dishwasher her partner is in the kitchen within moments, rearranging them to his specifications.*

Do any of these scenarios sound familiar? Some of us feel compelled to micromanage our partner's life. We scrutinize their habits or their language or their actions or their appearance and provide constant critical feedback. If you are a micromanager, you probably think you're doing your partner a favor. Ann-Beth's husband would tell us that she doesn't need those extra five pounds. Manny's girlfriend would say that she is trying to teach him the fine points of the English language. Hannah's partner would explain that you can wash more dishes at once if you load the dishwasher in a certain pattern. But are these explanations completely honest? Or is this really about "living your life according to me"?

Create Safe Spaces

When you are micromanaging your relationship, your partner can't relax and just be his or her natural self. It just isn't safe. Whether you realize it or not, your partner feels constantly judged. At first, this creates anxiety and discomfort; over time it creates resentment and separation. Does this sound like you're doing your partner a *favor*? Last time I checked, resentment and separation were not on the list of ingredients for a loving, effective partnership.

If you need to micromanage something, start by micromanaging your unhealthy impulses. Take time to figure out what is feeding your emotional responses to your partner's actions, appearance, preferences, etc. If you are committed to imposing your will onto your partner, you have to come to terms with your own control issues. Why does it always have to be *your* way? *Making it safe for your partner to relax and be human means learning to let go of control.*

CREATING SAFETY WITH RESPECTFUL BOUNDARIES

◆ *Maria loves her partner Cameron, but she hates the way he acts around her food. The moment Cameron finishes what he is eating, he shifts his focus to Maria's plate. "Are you going to eat that shrimp?""Do you want that french fry?""Are you going to finish your pudding?" Cameron is always ready to pounce on Maria's food and, not surprisingly, Maria can't enjoy her meal. She finds herself rushing to finish and anxiously defending the perimeter against Cameron's attacks. She also feels like a bad person for constantly pushing him away.*

◆ *Evie feels very close to Sam, but she complains that Sam feels a little too close. When Evie is on the phone, Sam is constantly hovering nearby. When the mail comes, Sam opens almost every piece, even personal letters that are addressed only to Evie. When Sam is short on cash, he will rummage through Evie's handbag without*

145

ever asking permission. Right now, Evie feels that the only way to keep Sam out of her very personal space is to take harsh counter-errorist measures such as hiding her handbag, locking herself in the bathroom when she's on the telephone, and diverting personal mail to a post office box. While she truly has nothing to hide, she still feels invaded by Sam's behavior. At the same time, she feels guilty for not being more tolerant and open.

Cameron and Sam have a lot to learn about respectful boundaries. They both regularly cross lines that push the limits of partnership, violating their partners' personal space and making things like the telephone, the mail, or the dinner table unsafe.

This lack of sensitivity to boundaries, illustrated in these stories, tends to be something that we inherit. If, for example, you grew up in a household where mealtime was a free-for-all, it can be hard to understand that your partner's food is not automatically *your* food, too. If you grew up in a household where physical space was in short supply, it can be hard to understand that your partner is entitled to a few feet of breathing room sometimes. If you grew up in a household where personal space was not respected—where your mail got opened, your drawers got opened, your diary got opened, etc.—it can be hard to grasp the whole concept of appropriate boundaries.

Our romantic history can also program us to have boundary issues. Maybe your last boyfriend *wanted* his life to read like an open book. Maybe your ex-wife *welcomed* your constant presence. Maybe your last lover *needed* to share every single detail of his or her life. That was fine for those relationships but those relationships are over, and it may not be so fine in the relationship you have now.

Creating safety in a relationship means recognizing and respecting all kinds of boundaries.

Most of us have become sensitive to how vital it is to respect sexual boundaries. And we have become sensitive to the crippling impact of crossing boundaries with violent physical behavior. But there are other boundary issues in relationships that require our attention, too. Creating safety means asking permission to cross more subtle personal lines and learning to ask questions like, "Is this something you want to share?" "Is it okay if I borrow this?" "Am I bothering you?" "Would you like me to go into a different room?" "Do you need some privacy?"

Feeling incredibly close to your partner doesn't automatically give you permission to ignore subtle personal boundaries. Creating safety in a relationship means accepting that you are a couple, not a commune.

CREATING SAFETY WITH FINANCIAL RESPONSIBILITY

We need to talk about money again. And it's okay to groan. But when you're trying to iron out the creases in the fabric of your relationship, there's just no getting around the impact of finances.

Perhaps right now you are feeling very good about money matters in your relationship. Maybe you have a working mini-merger. Or maybe you have a clear and acceptable separation of funds. But consider this: Almost everyone I speak to has a few blind spots in the area of financial responsibility, and these blind spots can wreak havoc on your partner's sense of safety in a relationship. *Let me give you some examples:*

- If you are carrying heavy credit card debt, this may be a source of serious anxiety for your partner, even if you keep your bills separate and *you* are certain your situation is "under control."
- If you are being chased by creditors your partner may be living in fear of answering the telephone, even if *you* are not intimidated by harassing phone calls and you assure your partner this is *your* responsibility.
- If you are financially *over*-responsible (*i.e.*, paranoid), you may be making it difficult for your partner to enjoy the slightest extravagance.

147

- If you are always borrowing money from your partner but never remembering to pay anything back (regardless of the sum), your casual attitude may be making your partner want to hide his/her available funds.

- If you pride yourself on your extreme sense of thrift, your partner may not feel safe to reveal the details of his/her daily purchases.

- If you are always ready to make huge financial commitments the moment you have some extra money, but you don't consider long-term scenarios and possible complications, your behavior may be making your partner squirm.

- If your eyes are bigger than your wallet—if you always want things you're not in a position to own—your partner may not feel it's safe to merge finances in any way.

- If you are always spending to your financial edges and your partner has a more conservative approach to money, your behavior may be giving him/her acid indigestion.

- If you are dodging the IRS because you're a little short of cash, your partner may be having regular nightmares about visiting you in prison.

Making the Smartest Relationship Investment

When you are single and unattached, you can do anything you want with your money. You can invest it wisely, spend it frivolously, bury it in the backyard, or burn it lighting your friend's cigars. But financial responsibility is a crucial factor in the partnership equation. You may still be keeping your financial matters completely separate, but you have to be sensitive to the impact of your attitudes and habits on your partner's psyche. As I said in the second chapter, you have to *talk* about money. You have to talk about your differences. You have to talk about your stressors. And whether you merge everything or nothing, you have to work together as a team to create a financial picture where both partners feel *safe*. That cooperation is the smartest investment you can make in your future as a couple.

TURNING YOUR ADMIRATION INTO AN ASSAULT

◆ *Annie knows that one of the main reasons she admires Ian is that he gave up a high-profile job in Washington, D.C., to start a small business at home because he felt it was more important to maintain balance in his life. Annie, on the other hand, is a workaholic who always feels the pressure from her corporate job. Last week Ian called Annie at work to tell her about an upsetting news story he had just heard on the radio while he was eating his breakfast. Annie, who had already been at her office for two hours quipped: "That happened four hours ago—but you were still fast asleep!"*

◆ *Robert, an attorney specializing in high-level mergers and acquisitions, is very proud of the fact that his wife Margo is an accomplished artist whose work has been purchased by several small museums. Margo is concerned that Robert's health has not been that good recently. Last Friday morning, as they were saying goodbye, Margo asked, "Why don't you take a sick day today?" Robert, in a voice that attempted to sound playful, responded, "Why don't you make some more money so you can support me?" Margo could clearly feel the edge beneath Robert's "playful" response.*

These two stories illustrate ways that we can make it unsafe for our partners to choose a different path, even when it is a path we admire. Understand this: Often, it is our own yearnings and shortcomings that shape our attraction to others. We are drawn to someone who is creative because we have trouble accessing our own creativity. We are drawn to someone who is emotionally effusive because we feel so bottled up. We are drawn to someone who works in the public sector because we secretly wish we could pursue a more noble path. We are drawn to someone who is very spiritual because we long for our own spiritual connection. These choices have the potential to enrich our lives; sometimes they even help us find those desirable parts within ourselves. But under stressful circumstances, qualities we secretly admire can become cannon fodder.

Making the relationship safe means taking responsibility for your own insecurities, yearnings, missed opportunities, self-doubt, and envy. When we punish our partner for having qualities we desire we hurt their spirit, we hurt our own hopes for growth and change, and we hurt the possibilities for partnership.

ARE YOU HOLDING YOUR PARTNER "HOSTAGE"?

One of our neighbors, having recently learned that I write books about relationships, has been trying to impress me ever since with his own relationship savvy. And he loves to tell stories that illustrate this savvy.

"My wife can get pretty insecure sometimes," a recent story of his began. "Last week she asked me, 'Do I make you happy?' I tried to ignore the question," he continued, "but she asked again. Finally I said to her straight out, 'When there's a big problem, I'll let you know.' I thought that was a very honest answer." Then he looked at me for some kind of acknowledgment.

"If I were your wife," I responded, "I would feel like I was being held hostage."

One of the easiest mistakes to make in a relationship is not seeing the ways in which we are holding our partner hostage. My neighbor, for example, is holding his wife hostage by witholding information until *he* decides it's "a big problem." His wife has to wait, and worry about what he means by "big," and what he will do when that line has been crossed. For her, the relationship *never* feels very safe.

Six More "Typical" Hostage Scenarios

Witholding vital relationship information is just one of the ways we can hold a partner hostage. Here are a few other classic "hostage" scenarios:

◆ *Blake has something negative to say about every restaurant he and his wife Lonni visit. The service is terrible. The kitchen looks dirty. The owner looks like a criminal. The mayonnaise looks weird. The food is always cold. The air-conditioner isn't cold enough. And so on. Blake's attitude makes it really difficult for Lonni to ever enjoy a meal out. She has reached the point where she would rather just stay home and let Blake cook every night.*

◆ *Alexander is sitting at home with his girlfriend Yvette, and he has just started reading the newspaper. "What are you reading about?" Yvette will ask. Alexander will answer her politely, and try to continue reading, but soon Yvette will ask, "Did you work in the garden today?" Alexander will nod, and try to continue reading. "I heard the strangest story at work this morning. . . ," Yvette begins. At this point, Alexander realizes he will never be able to just relax and quietly read the paper. He loves Yvette, but he is exhausted by her peskiness.*

◆ *Dee-Dee is sitting in her car in the driveway of her house feeling reluctant to leave the car and go inside. She had a really positive day at her new sales job and she doesn't want to ruin her good mood. The potential "mood ruiner" is Carver, Dee-Dee's partner. Carver is a really good guy, and very loving, but he is almost always immersed in some personal crisis. Sometimes it's a medical emergency, sometimes it's a work emergency, sometimes it's a money crisis, and sometimes it's family drama—but it's always* something. *Dee-Dee resents the fact that her good feelings are probably going to be swept aside by Carver's crisis-du-jour.*

◆ *Fifteen minutes ago, Danny checked his e-mail and discovered a very upsetting message from his girlfriend Rena. The message read, "Something completely horrible just happened here. Call me at the office." Danny tried to reach Rena immediately but he kept getting connected to her voice mail. Worst-case scenarios raced through his mind. A moment later, Danny finally got Rena on the phone. "Are you okay?" Danny asked. "I'm fine," Rena responded casually. "What happened?," he pressed. "Oh . . ." Rena answered, finally realizing what he was referring to, "there was a mouse in the lunch-room." Danny is relieved that Rena is okay. But he's also angry that she has caused him unnecessary worry with her vague, dramatic e-mail. While this isn't new behavior for Rena, it's behavior Danny still can't get used to.*

◆ *Arthur swears he would never ever use physical force in his relationship with Bette. Yet he is using it around his relationship constantly. He pounds his fists on the table when he gets into a heated telephone conversation. He kicks the wastebasket when he's in a bad mood. And yesterday he threw his keys across the room when he found out how much it was going to cost to replace his car's transmission. Arthur has never ever directed this anger at Bette, but Bette still feels terrified by his behavior.*

◆ *Stephanie likes Tim's children from his first marriage, but she can't stand that they make such a mess when they come for the weekend. She never says anything, but she grimaces and makes faces, and her general unhappiness casts a pall over the entire apartment. This is so upsetting to Tim that he is thinking of moving out. The apartment doesn't feel like a safe environment for himself or his children.*

Creating Safe Spaces Means
Releasing Your Hostages

Whining, complaining, annoying, or witholding. Being moody, being unpredictable, being overly dramatic, or being out of control. These are just *some* of the ways we make the relationship feel unsafe. Your partner is the perfect hostage—someone who loves you, cares about you, and wants to be with you. But someone who loves you, cares about you, and wants to be with you is also someone who can be taken advantage of. And that is exactly what happens sometimes—we take advantage of our partner's willingness to *be* a partner, subjecting them to an unhealthy helping of whatever it is we're in the mood to dish out. Taking advantage of your partner's good intentions is selfish and shortsighted. It may feel good in the moment, but it does not encourage closeness and connection.

Creating safe spaces means . . .

- not trying to impose your mood on your partner.
- being more predictable.
- not resorting to subtle intimidation.
- not using angry body language to control others.
- finding another ear (ideally, a therapist's or counselor's ear) to hear about your ongoing distress.
- making a concerted effort to be more positive.
- giving your partner some breathing room.
- understanding that your feelings don't always take center stage.
- cleaning up your eggshells so your partner can walk around you with comfort.
- getting a handle on your rage.

CREATING SAFETY BY TAKING YOUR ANGER SERIOUSLY

By the time most of us are lucky enough to find our way into a loving, stable relationship, we are likely to have with us some very powerful fantasies about what it will feel like to have an argument with our "dream" partner. Some people, for example, are convinced that they should "never, ever go to bed angry." Some people imagine that every heated exchange will end with an hour of frantic of lovemaking. Some people are confident that all of their relationship wisdom will guide them through the choppiest channels without an emotional bruise. And some people fantasize that there will never *be* an argument because they will be experiencing such perfect accord. Then reality comes, and these fantasies are put to the test.

Anger makes most of us very uncomfortable. It makes some of us so uncomfortable that we do everything in our power to avoid it, make light of it, or drive it underground and deny its existence. Yet if there is one thing you can count on in a loving, long-term relationship, it is the eventual arrival of some angry moments. The way those moments are handled is one of the most dramatic influences on our sense of safety in the relationship. And this is where it becomes so critical for the survival of your relationship to be fighting the fair fight.

Repeating Old Patterns, Fighting the Old Family Fight

So many of us are using our current relationships as an arena to fight the old family fight. Often, we can't even see that we are repeating distancing and destructive ways of "doing battle" we learned in the households we grew up in. Consider these examples . . .

Create Safe Spaces

◆ When Esther was a child, her parents fought a lot. Whenever Esther's mother would get really angry at Esther's father she would snap at him, "I don't love you right now!" Today, when Esther gets angry at her boyfriend she says the exact same thing to him, unable to imagine how hurtful her words are.

◆ Eddie comes from a large (five brothers), noisy family that had their arguments at maximum strength and volume. Eddie feels that there's nothing wrong with going on a loud rant once in a while, as long as he apologizes to his partner later.

◆ Ellis swears he never saw his parents fight. What he did see was two people trying to control each other with silence and angry glares. Ellis prides himself on the fact that he has never raised his voice at his wife, but his wife experiences Ellis's harsh silences as punishing.

◆ Gwynneth comes from an alcoholic household where she watched her mother get drunk and get mean, and watched her father absorb the assault the best he could. Though it makes Gwynneth feel awful to see herself acting like her mother, that doesn't always stop her from taking a mean swipe at her partner.

◆ Georgia grew up in a household where her father rarely raised his voice, but regularly showed his anger by going around the house slamming doors. Today, Georgia acts just like her father did, sending angry messages through the house by banging dishes, slamming drawers shut, and generally making loud angry noises.

◆ Trent's father was a terribly chauvinistic man who never took his wife's feelings seriously. Trent has tried very hard to be a more "evolved" partner, but whenever his fiancée gets angry at him, the first thing he says is, "Did you just get your period?"

What is *your* fighting style? Is it something you "inherited" from the examples that surrounded you in your childhood? Most of us don't take the time to stop, look back, and consider how much of our family legacy we have brought forward into the relationship "ring."

Do you come from a family where fights were particularly mean-spirited, or do you come from a family where fights were not allowed? Do you come from a family where verbal assaults were considered affectionate? Do you come from a family where attacks were delivered through sweet-voiced barbs? Do you come from a family where someone was always having a tantrum, or do you come from a family where everyone was trying to control each other with stares and glares? Do you come from a family where the fighting never stopped—where fighting was just a way of life? Do you come from a family where people were out of control? *How has this history affected your personal fighting style?*

If You Want to Shed Family Baggage, It Helps to Open the Bags

Ask yourself these questions . . .

- When it comes to having a fight with your partner, are you a carbon copy of your parents?
- Do you fight with your partner the way you always fought with your siblings?
- Have you taken a vow to never fight at all because it was so intolerable in your childhood?
- Do you assume that your style of fighting is *safe* for your partner because you survived it in your own family?

If you fight with your partner the way you fought with your parents or siblings, or the way your parents fought with each other, it's easy to assume that you're fighting a fair fight. After all, this may be the only fighting style that you know or understand. But that doesn't make it safe.

Very few families can be held up as fine models for fair fighting. And while you may feel *comfortable* with your particular fighting style because it's so familiar, you may be creating extraordinary discomfort for your partner and sabotaging your chances for a productive partnership. We all want to think that when we have a fight with our partner we're doing it in an appropriate, fair, and *safe* manner. But the biggest mistake a person can make is to assume that he or she is fighting the fair fight just because it has the family stamp of approval.

Only your partner can tell you if you are fighting the fair fight. Only your partner can tell you whether or not he/she experiences you as *safe*; you aren't qualified to judge.

REPRESSING YOUR ANGER DOES NOT MAKE A RELATIONSHIP SAFE

I have spoken to more than a few men and women who tell me that they have never had a single argument with their partners. Yet I always come away from these conversations feeling uncomfortable. Perhaps it is because I'm painfully aware of how unexpressed anger can be so much more destructive than anger that's expressed in a healthy way.

When anger isn't welcome in a relationship, for whatever reason, it's going to appear in some other form. And as I say this, I can't help thinking about the following individuals who I have known . . .

There is, for example, Waldo, who never expresses his anger at his wife, but who regularly finds himself fantasizing about having an affair. There is Eva, who would never admit her anger to her boyfriend, but starts eating the moment she's upset—and then hates *herself* for being fifteen pounds overweight. There is Ernest, who never feels much anger, but is constantly struggling with depression. And there are Cedric and Willa, who contain their anger and disagreements with chronic marijuana use.

These are not healthy scenarios. Some of these people are completely out of touch with their anger, and others are unwilling to express their anger directly, but as I hope you can clearly see, the anger is taking its toll. Repressing your anger is not how you make your partner feel safe. To make your partner feel safe you need to have a healthy respect for your anger, a healthy respect for your partner's anger, and a commitment to working with that anger in honest, constructive ways that are *never* abusive or intentionally threatening. Creating a successful partnership requires a willingness to live with the discomfort of very intense emotions.

FIGHTING TO THE POINT OF NO RETURN

Joli and Seth are in the middle of a really upsetting argument about the way Seth sometimes puts his parents' needs before the needs of his relationship with Joli. Joli is feeling exhausted by this argument, and as it heats up, she starts thinking to herself, "Life was so much easier when I was single." Then she makes a classic relationship blunder. She turns to Seth and says out loud, "Maybe we should just end *this relationship."*

Joli is hoping for a reassuring response from Seth. She wants him to back down and tell her how much she means to him. But Seth is feeling attacked and defensive. And he is also exhausted from this fight. So he responds, "Maybe we should."

Joli's heart starts to sink. Confused by Seth's response, and still feeling very angry, she answers back, "Maybe we should."

This may be the final moment in a fundamentally good relationship because Joli and Seth have fought themselves into a corner they may not be able to escape from. And this is a painful lesson: ***Fighting the fair fight means NEVER using a breakup as your bargaining chip.***

Many great relationships have ended with conversations like this one. Sometimes it happens because one or both partners *want* the relationship to end. But many more times it happens because one partner is gambling that they can scare the other into being more responsive, or because one partner has made the terrible mistake of letting anger overpower his or her ability to protect the sanctity of the relationship.

It is very easy to go over the top when you are fighting with your partner. A person who loves you and wants to be with you is usually going to put up with a lot more than someone who is marginally interested, indifferent, or just looking for an excuse to bolt. But our partner's love can also give us a sense of safety that we take advantage of. We say and do things that we would never say or do to anyone else—we reveal extremes that we keep carefully hidden from the outside world. And sometimes, we go too far.

How do you insure that important arguments don't turn into ugly, relationship-threatening events? It helps if you have a realistic sense of your own power. And it helps if you are always trying to understand your partner's vulnerability. Your partner may not be as emotionally strong or emotionally resilient as you. Furthermore, the two of you may have different areas of vulnerability. It is always a mistake to assume that your partner can handle anything you can handle.

FIGHTING THE FAIR FIGHT: THE RULES

It is very hard not to sound like a teacher or a concerned parent when I'm talking about this crucial relationship material. But, risking that, I encourage you with all my sincerity to take the following suggestions to heart . . .

Fighting the fair fight means . . .

- *never* resorting to threats or intimidation.
- never being intentionally hurtful.

THIS IS HOW LOVE WORKS

- understanding that your words are powerful weapons.
- never having punishment as your goal.
- always giving your partner equal time to speak his or her peace.
- never assuming you are 100 percent in the right.
- not acting out your anger with undermining behaviors (flirting with someone else, disappearing, etc.)
- not bringing other people's opinions into your argument.
- not using manipulation to get the results you want.
- never involving your children or stepchildren in your arguments.
- never taking potshots at things your partner can't change.
- overcoming your need to always take the last verbal swing.
- not saving up your anger till it reaches critical mass.
- being willing to apologize sincerely, even when you are clear it was not your "fault."

SECRET #7:

Support Each Other's Dreams

． ◆ ．

◆ *Tracy has gone back to college to get a B.A. in order to fulfill her dream of becoming a teacher. While she is doing this, she will be earning less money; this will make a significant difference in the family income. To make it all work, Tracy needs the full support of her husband, Nathan.*

◆ *Barry, Marilyn, and their young daughter have been living in a small two-bedroom apartment for the past five years. Marilyn is not unhappy in this apartment, but Barry desperately wants to save enough money to make a down payment on a modest house; he has lived in apartments his whole life, and owning a house is his dream. To make this possible, Marilyn is going to have to make as many financial sacrifices as Barry.*

Most of us are familiar with these "turning dreams into reality" scenarios. As unattached singles, we often fantasized about supporting our partners while they pursued their dreams; and we imagined what it would be like to be with good-natured, loving partners who believed in *our* dreams. When we finally find a relationship, however, we often discover something very real: to make a partnership work, dreams require serious cooperation.

DREAMING IN THE REAL WORLD

When Jill and I married in 1996, my first priority became helping her realize one of her most important dreams—to be in business for herself. I entered into this voluntarily, knowing that Jill was prepared to wait many more years if that was necessary, or sacrifice the dream entirely if a good opportunity never presented itself. But seeing so clearly how strongly Jill felt made it very difficult for me to ignore her hopes. From the very first time she shared this dream with me—maybe six months into our relationship—her dream started becoming my dream, too. By the time we were married, our first opportunity appeared to make this dream come true.

When I tell people this story, their reaction is always the same. Every face conveys admiration and approval, and people are quick to praise me with comments such as, "That is so loving" or "You're such a supportive partner" or "I can only hope that one day I'll have a relationship like yours." Perhaps you're having similar thoughts, too. Perhaps this makes you think of dreams of your own that you have been reluctant to confess to your partner because it's so scary to ask for support. But if you think I'm sharing this story with you just to show you what a terrific partner and terrific human being I am, let me warn you now that I haven't finished the story.

Turning Jill's dream into a reality became a two-and-a-half-year project that organized the beginning of our marriage, and, in many ways, consumed it. With all of the payoffs you might expect—with all of the feelings of love and support and unity—also came an endless supply of struggles, questions, problems, and yes, occasional bouts of genuine unhappiness and regret. After one year, money got very tight. Budgets were readjusted, vacation plans were canceled, and Jill's demanding new work schedule left me periodically feeling cheated and abandoned. I was certainly happy to bask in the glory of being a prince among men, but I was completely unprepared for the negatives and this lack of preparedness cost me a piece of my hide. Much of this embarrasses me, but I am sharing it with you because it is a big piece of reality that you need to be prepared for if you are going to stand up for your partner's dreams.

There is a huge difference between having good intentions and being able to survive the process of implementing those intentions, particularly when that process consumes years of your life. In those two and a half years, I learned some very hard lessons about taking on your partner's dreams. I had to confront my own selfishness and naiveté. I had to suffer through the unexpected loss of deferring or abandoning many of my own dreams. I had to learn what it *really* means to be a partner; I had to learn what it means to not just *want* to do the right thing, but to actually do it—to follow through from start to finish. And I had to learn that my fantasy skills were far more well-honed than my reality skills.

Needless to say, I was not the only one in our marriage getting this first-class education. It was, for both of us, a stretching exercise that challenged us on every level. Yet through this process we also learned, albeit it in the most difficult way at times, how crucial it is in a loving partnership to be willing and able to support each other's dreams.

In a partnership, the focus, strength, and commitment of two people working together as a team can create possibilities that are unattainable for just one person acting alone. In an effective partnership, the loving whole has much greater power and potential than its individual parts.

FINDING A DREAM WORTH SUPPORTING: DREAMING SINGLE vs. DREAMING PARTNERED

Both people in a relationship arrive at that relationship with a variety of personal and professional dreams. But these dreams are usually the product of dreaming single—they are dreams that took shape in the absence of a solid partnership.

So the big question is this: How do these dreams hold up in the world of loving partnership? To put it more bluntly: Do these dreams support the concept of partnership, or do they fuel the mechanism of *separation?*

Some dreams are obviously bad for a partnership and need to be packed away with other single-life memorabilia. Dreams such as chucking it all and hitchhiking across the country, taking your life savings to Las Vegas and trying to double your money, spending your last dime on a brand new Ferrari, or having a ménage-à-trois with your next-door-neighbors. But far more often this process of sorting out the important dreams from the not-so-important dreams, and the workable dreams from the unworkable dreams, can get very complicated.

◆ *Deni has always dreamed of writing and shooting her own low-budget feature film. Now that she is married to Victor, and they are a two-income family, she has the extra money to make this possible. But making this dream a reality means many other demands, including at least two years of very late nights at the office for Deni and another six months of shooting on location without Victor. Then there is the post-production nightmare, demanding even more time from Deni. Will their relationship be able to survive the strain?*

◆ *Sandy has always dreamed of buying an old Victorian-style fixer-upper and spending all of his free time turning it into a little gem. Sandy's partner Jo has just received a small inheritance that would cover the down payment on a house like this. But the idea of living in a house that has to be completely gutted and rebuilt is completely unsettling and fills her with dread. Jo works at a frantic pace all day, and she needs a place to come home to every night where she can feel cradled and cared for. Is this fixer-upper really such a good idea?*

◆ *Ellie has always dreamed of owning a golden retriever, but she never got one because she can't get home in time to walk a dog in the early evening. Now that Ellie is living with Fisk, the possibility of getting a dog has been reawakened. Fisk is always at home in the late afternoon, and he would have the time to walk the dog. There's only one problem: Fisk is allergic to most dogs, particularly long-haired dogs. Is Ellie's dream more important than Fisk's uncomfortable allergies?*

◆ *Sean has studied the stock market for years and always dreamed of being "a player," but he has never had the extra money to make the kind of investments that would pay off in a big way. Now, however, he and his new bride Keesha have almost $15,000 in cash that came from wedding gifts. Sean is chomping at the bit. He feels confident he could triple that $15,000 within one year. But Keesha is not happy. She is tired of always worrying about money and security, and she thinks this gift money should be put in the bank and left untouched so the couple has something substantial to handle serious financial emergencies. Is Sean's dream more important than Keesha's concerns?*

These four couples are about to learn the difference between "dreaming single" and "dreaming partnered." A dream is only viable and worth the support of both partners if it is a dream that is good for both of them. In other words, *an individual dream has to survive the transition to a "group dream" for it to be a positive partnership dream.* Deni's dream does not account for some basic relationship needs, and it could prove to be destructive if it is not seriously modified to minimize long separations and accommodate other relationship realities. Sandy might have to find a Victorian house that is a lot more liveable on move-in day, and abandon some of his more ambitious dreams if his partner is going to find the relationship liveable after move-in day. Ellie may need to get a poodle or sacrifice this one dream entirely. And Sean may have to wait until the couple has built a much bigger nest egg before he can think about risking any portion of that money in the highly volatile stock market. These are the very real and important ramifications of dreaming partnered.

SPRINKLING SOME REALITY ON BIG DREAMS

If living your dream is going to threaten the integrity of your relationship, it is not a loving dream.

If helping your partner live his or her dream is going to threaten the integrity of your relationship, it is not a dream you should be supporting.

Not every dream is meant to be, and not every dream deserves the full support of both partners. Sometimes the timing is bad. Sometimes the design is flawed. Sometimes it involves too much risk for a couple to take on. Sometimes it was meant to be just a fantasy. Regardless of where the dream had its origins—in your mind or in the mind of your partner—the dream has to work for *both* of you now.

A dream worth supporting . . .

- has to work for everyone's budget.
- has to work for everyone's schedule.
- has to work for everyone's personality.
- has to work for everyone's interests.
- has to work for everyone's psyche.
- has to work for everyone's life.

Old Dreams Do Not Always Suit
the New Reality of Partnership

A viable dream has to be one that makes sense for the partnership.
That is the only kind of dream that deserves complete support. When
we find a stable, loving relationship our world changes. Sometimes it
changes dramatically, and our old dreams do not suit this new reality. If we try to force these old, "single" dreams upon our partner we
are either ignoring the new reality, or trying to sabotage it (a process
that is not always conscious). Either way, our old dreams can steer the
relationship in a dangerous direction. *Sometimes building a partnership
means finding new dreams.*

JOINING THE TEAM,
SUPPORTING THE DREAM

Are you a team player? Before your "dreamwork" begins, you need to
ask yourself this question—particularly if you have spent many years
being single and unattached. Most of us know what it means to function as part of an effective team. We have done it on the playing field.
And we have done it at the office. We know all the team jargon, and we
can usually muster team spirit. Yet when it comes to our personal life,
we easily forget the lessons of teamwork we have learned in other areas
of our life. Without a coach to keep us on track, it's not unusual to drift
apart and start playing by rules that do not support partnership.

To be in a relationship where dreams are supported, both members
of that partnership must be willing to sacrifice their maverick behavior for the good of the couple—for the good of the team. Otherwise,
your experience of relationship will never be more than the experience of two people always wrestling to put their personal goals and
needs and fantasies at the top of the pile. Partnership is not an exer-

cise in, "Give me the ball and let me run with it because I'm faster or better or smarter or wiser or more experienced or more in need or more *whatever* than you." *Standing up for each other's dreams means living by this powerful motto: "We are going to do this together, or we are not going to do it at all."*

Do you have what it takes to help turn your relationship into a *"dream team"*—a partnership where both individuals are working in a loving, respectful, and coordinated way to support each other's dreams? Consider some of these non-negotiable teamwork fundamentals . . .

The Nine Rules of Teamwork

1) You have to take turns.
2) If you're not committed to crossing the finish line, don't cross the starting line.
3) You don't get to quit just because *you* are tired or bored.
4) Big decisions are team decisions.
5) Take lots of time-outs to reevaluate.
6) Be sure this is a victory you can handle before you join the team.
7) Remember whose team you are on.
8) Keep your personal agenda in check.
9) Nobody wins unless everybody wins.

1. You have to take turns.

Sometimes a couple's dreams are in such perfect synch that their desires get taken care of at the exact same time. She dreams of a long warm-weather vacation, he dreams of going to cooking school, and *voilá*, they're both happy campers in the south of France. He dreams of having a bigger kitchen, she dreams of having more closets, and suddenly the larger apartment next door becomes available and they both get their wish. But it usually *doesn't* work this way, and that means you have to be willing to take turns.

Maybe this year the focus is on getting you that new computer you want so desperately, and next year the focus is on converting your garage to an office for your partner. Maybe this year the focus is on paying down your partner's credit card bills and next year the focus will be on starting the family vacation you've been dreaming about. But if you're not willing to trade off in a completely fair and balanced way, you're not ready to be a dream team.

While most people understand the concept of taking turns, it's my experience that many aren't very good at embracing the true spirit of this concept and putting it into practice. For example, we say we're going to take turns, but we insist on always going first and don't stay committed to our partner's dreams. Or we continue to put our partner's needs above our own, chronically deferring our own dreams. Neither of these lead to good feelings in a partnership.

Taking turns means accepting that your dreams aren't any more valid than your partner's dreams, they're just different. And you don't always get to go first. (That means you have to be a good sport.) Taking turns also means taking your own dreams seriously, and not becoming resentful by always putting aside these dreams in the service of your partner's dreams.

2. If you're not committed to crossing the finish line, don't cross the starting line.

Here is a big mistake that a lot of very well-intentioned people make: They get so caught up in their partner's hopes that they neglect the larger picture. They don't make a plan. They don't make a back-up plan. They don't sweat the details. They don't sit down with their partner and brainstorm their way through best-case and worst-case scenarios. They are there on "launch day" with 1,000 percent enthusiasm, but they have no interest in hanging around at "mission control" long after the exciting launch to see everything through and offer *consistent* support.

There is a huge difference between encouraging your partner to pursue a dream and working with your partner to see that dream through. And your powerful enthusiasm can quickly become "the problem" if your commitment is not equally powerful. "Why did you encourage me?" your partner asks. "It would have been easier if this never got started."

Standing up for your partner's dreams may be harder than you expect or easier than you expect, but it will almost never be exactly what you expect. So before you get started you need to be clear that you're in this for the long haul. If you're not sure that you are in 100 percent—prepared to deal with the ups *and* the downs—it's better to wait. This is something you can not be casual or cavalier about. Your *enthusiasm* is certainly important, but your partner needs your *commitment* more. Once the "dream door" is opened, slamming it shut has considerable emotional costs.

3. You don't get to quit just because YOU are tired or bored.

- ◆ *Jasmine was really excited about the idea of moving with her boyfriend Francis to San Francisco so he could take a better job, but she's finding it difficult to deal with new neighbors, a new house, new friends for her kids, etc. She's getting tired of all the adjustments and starting to make noises about moving back to Ohio.*
- ◆ *Emanuel promised to help his wife paint the kitchen this summer, but halfway into the process he's feeling overwhelmed, cranky, and ready to throw in the towel.*

Both Emanuel and Jasmine are about to break a fundamental rule of teamwork. As my own story earlier in this chapter illustrated, dreams don't always come true as quickly and efficiently as we hope. Sometimes they demand far more time than you may have ever imagined. Sometimes they demand far more energy than you may have ever imagined. Sometimes they demand far more money than you may have ever imagined. Sometimes they demand far more of an emotional investment than you may have ever imagined. And sometimes, they demand all of the above. This means that there is a very good chance that at least one of you is going to feel depleted before this process is complete—and it's probably going to be *you*, the supportive one, because you are less vested in the dream.

Does that mean it's okay to quit? Absolutely not. *You can't give a dream lip service if you're not going to give it full service.*

Imagine what it would be like if every team athlete could pack up and go home in the middle of the game because he or she was feeling frustrated or scared or tired. That's not the way team play works. *If you are going to stand up for each other's dreams, you start as a team and you finish as a team, even if you finish short of your goals.* Individual problems may come up—anxiety, doubt, regret, uncertainty—but these issues are now a *team* problem that the team solves as a unit. Both of you are entitled to struggle, but it has to be a shared struggle. Both of you are certainly entitled to quit, but only if you quit *as a team*. And that leads me to the next team fundamental . . .

4. Big decisions are team decisions.

After almost a year of dating, Josia and Faith have decided that it's time to move in together. They are both excited, but they also have very different ideas about finding a place to live. Faith, who is always feeling strapped for cash, has been thinking, "If we can find something modest this is our big chance to start saving some money, and maybe even pay down debts from graduate school." She's already combing the classified ads for inexpensive rentals. Josia, who has always been unhappy living in a small apartment, has been thinking, "This is our first chance to combine our spending power and get a really great place to live." He has already started driving around upscale neighborhoods looking for vacancies.

Josia and Faith don't know it yet, but their living-together dream scenarios are about to collide and their capacity for partnership is about to be put to the test in a big way. No one partner is right or wrong here; both dream scenarios are valid. But Josia and Faith are going to come out of their separate corners and work with each other for *any* dream to be fulfilled. Their ability to respect each other's dreams, talk through all of their options, and make a good decision *as a team* is going to have a huge influence on the future of their relationship.

When it comes to turning dreams into reality, big decisions have to be made as a team. It doesn't really matter how or where the dream began; it doesn't really matter who brought this dream into the relationship. Once the actual process begins, it's *everyone's* dream. That's the only way it's going to work. Both Josia and Faith have to have the same goals, even if those goals reflect a lot of compromise. And both need to have an equal voice in achieving those goals. That's what it means to be an effective dream team.

5. Take lots of time-outs to reevaluate.

It starts with a dream. But as soon as we take our very first steps to bring that dream to life, stuff happens. Real life is always going to adjust, modify, and complicate even the simplest dreams. You need to be discussing these twists and turns regularly and revising your strategy if necessary. And the only way to do that is to have regular "time-outs."

Ask any architect to tell you about the difference between a brilliant set of plans and a completed, fully functioning building. Ask any CEO to explain the difference between a breakthrough idea and a money-making business based on that idea. Ask any film producer to talk about the difference between a brilliant script and a finished movie. The universe has its own rules, and those rules can and *will* change like the wind. If you are not constantly re-evaluating and reworking your plans—*as a team*—to accommodate those changes, you're not working as a team. It's part of the nuts-and-bolts procedure that makes it possible for dreams to really come true.

Sometimes real life is going to completely thwart your best attempts to turn a dream into a reality. When you are regularly taking time-outs, you are also giving your team the chance to acknowledge dream-breaking problems and make intelligent decisions about the future. There is no shame in making a team decision to give up on a dream that's just not meant to be right now. As far as the survival of your relationship is concerned, the riskier thing is investing time, energy, hope, or money on a dream because you can't stop and have an honest conversation about what isn't working.

6. *Be sure this is a victory you can handle before you join the team.*

Okay, you want to be a decent partner and you want to do the right thing. But are you really up for the emotional fallout of your team's *success*? How will you feel when the dream you're supporting becomes a reality? It's very easy to go through the motions of being a supportive partner, but it's also easy to neglect or bury your own *personal* needs and sensitivities in the process, and end up with a nightmare you can't handle.

Will, for example, helping your partner go back to school for a degree make you jealous because you never got *your* degree? Will helping your partner buy a new car make you resentful because you're still driving an old clunker? Will supporting your partner's dream to buy a home make you chronically anxious because that mortgage has to be paid on time every month? Will supporting your partner's dream to write a novel make you insecure when your partner starts getting public attention? Will helping your partner's bid for public office make you angry because he/she is never home?

Before you throw your support behind your partner's dreams, you need to think through the details of the process and the possible *emotional* consequences at every stage of this process, *including the victory*

173

THIS IS HOW LOVE WORKS

THIS IS HOW LOVE WORKS

stage. How could the success of this dream play into your jealousy, your envy, your insecurity, your competitiveness, and your fear? Could this dream turn into your personal nightmare—something you wish you could destroy? You are not doing your partner a favor if you're encouraging a process that leaves you smoldering with unpleasant emotional baggage. Instead of feeling bad because you're not up for the consequences of a victory, try to understand *why* you're not up for those consequences. You are certainly entitled to your feelings, and you're not a bad partner for having these feelings. Talking through your greatest fears and concerns may be all you need to dismantle them, particularly if your partner can give you the reassurance you require.

7. Remember whose team you are on.

♦ *Farrell promised his partner Zoe that he would do everything he could to help her pay for her last semester of graduate school this year so she could stop working temp jobs and focus on her studies. But last week Farrell's grown son from his first marriage pleaded with him for a long-term loan for a new car and Farrell caved in, giving up most of the money he was planning to give Zoe. Zoe is furious. It's not like his son had a real emergency. How could Farrell have let Zoe get her hopes up so high and then do this?*

♦ *China and Bobby have just finished planning their first trip to Ireland. This is Bobby's first chance to see the village where both his grandparents were born, a dream he has had for a long time. Bobby has been sacrificing many small pleasures to save up the money he needs to make this trip possible. But China is already having second thoughts. While China has already been to Europe twice, her mother has never traveled outside of the United States—she has never even traveled outside of California. China's guilt is making her think that Bobby's dream trip may be too frivolous right now. As he listens to China talk about this, Bobby's heart starts to sink.*

Support Each Other's Dreams

◆ *After planning this for more than a month, Isabel has just spent all day preparing her very first Thanksgiving dinner for her husband Clark, his sister, his parents, and his two children from a previous marriage. Clark has been a great support, but when the doorbell rings on Thanksgiving Day that quickly changes. When Clark's sister arrives the first thing she says to Clark is, "Do you have anything besides turkey? It makes me sleepy these days." Clark immediately assures her that he can make her a steak. Clark's mother looks disapprovingly at the turkey and says, "I forgot to give Isabel my recipe." Clark responds, "You certainly do make an amazing turkey, Mom." Isabel tells herself that next year she will order Thanksgiving dinner from a restaurant.*

Under pressure from family or friends, Farrell, China, and Clark have all forgotten whose team they are on. And this mistake is a common one. It's easy to support our partner's dreams in a vacuum, but what happens when voices from outside your team challenge your support? What happens when your partner's dream elicits disapproval, criticism, or laughter from someone else you respect? What happens when your desire to be supportive leaves you feeling torn between your partner and some other important figure in your life, such as your best friend, your business partner, or your boss? Standing up for your partner's dreams will never work if you can't stand up for your partner. You may have many very important people in your life, but you have only one partner. If you want to make sure that message gets across, you can't play on more than one side.

8. Keep your personal agenda in check.

Seven years ago, when I first met my wife, one of my greatest dreams was to learn to paint, and I shared this information with Jill very early in our relationship. Our first Christmas together as a couple, Jill took a considerable chunk of her hard-earned money and bought me a mag-

175

nificent wooden easel. I was completely surprised by the gift, and over-whelmed by the clear message of support in this gift—a message that said, "I believe in your dream." But one year later I had still not opened the box and assembled the easel. *Two* years later I had still not opened the box. *Three* years later, the box remained sealed. I was still not ready.

During these years, Jill *never* made me feel uncomfortable about the fact that I had so much resistance to my own dream. She never made jokes about the unopened box. She never expressed regret about spending so much money. She never questioned my intentions or abilities as an artist. She never did *anything* to change her message of support. I don't know why Jill chose this particular dream of mine to be the very first one to support. But if Jill had a personal agenda that was different from mine, she never let it show. This is what it means to *not* impose your personal agenda on your partner's dream.

I think it's important for all of us to acknowledge that when we make the decision to stand up for one of our partner's dreams, that decision is not always going to come from a place of 100-percent pure goodwill and love. Sometimes your support will be influenced by your own hopes and dreams ("I've always wanted this too!"). Sometimes you're searching for reciprocal support ("One day it's going to be *my* turn!"). Sometimes you can see big potential payoffs that go beyond the emotional payoff of strengthening your connection ("We'll have more money to go out to dinner!"). Sometimes you're just trying to do the right thing. The important thing is to keep your agenda from interfering with your partner's dream. **Your partner should never feel pressured by your support.**

9. Nobody wins unless everybody wins.

You have heard this many times, so I'm not going to belabor the point: A dream worth supporting is a dream where both partners in the relationship will have a clear sense of victory. Sometimes that sense of victory comes from something very concrete (a new job, a new car, a new garden, a new puppy), and sometimes it comes from an emotional payoff such as sharing your partner's joy. But it has to come from *somewhere*.

Too many dreams are win-lose dreams—what I call "good news/bad news dreams." For one partner, the result is a dream-come-true. That's the "good news." But for the other partner, the sacrifice has been too great, and at the end there is jealousy, resentment, or some other bad feeling (the "bad news").

Remember this: You're supporting each other's dreams in the spirit of love, but you're also supporting each other's dreams in the spirit of partnership. Both of these elements are vital. *Being a martyr does NOT make you a good partner. Neither does pushing for your dreams at your partner's expense.*

THE IMPORTANCE OF SMALLER DREAMS

Not all dreams are large. Not all dreams involve huge houses, big projects, elaborate trips, and giant sums of cash. But that doesn't diminish their importance. Little dreams can have an big impact on partnership because they test our ability to tune in to our partner's ever-changing emotional needs and concerns. Here are some typical examples of the more modest kinds of dreams that become important in the negotiation of partnership:

◆ *Marianne says that all she wants from Gregg is that he understands how important it is to her to keep the guest bathroom looking clean. Why, she asks, does he inevitably track his dirty shoes over the bathroom rug the minute she has finished cleaning it?*

◆ *Matt says that all he asks from Jennie is that they have just one holiday dinner with his family without her getting into a huge fight with his sister.*

◆ Bob says that all he wants from his wife is that she understand that when he comes home from work he needs to unwind for half an hour before he hears about, or has to take on, any new projects around the house.

◆ Marda says that all she asks of her husband is that he understand how hard it is for her to get their newborn baby to go to sleep at night, and that when he works late, he stop going in to the baby's room when he gets home and purposely waking her up.

When Marianne, Matt, Bob, and Marda say "This is what I really want," they mean it. Someday, they too may be more focused on larger dreams like a change of career or a change of residence, but right now, these more modest dreams are the dreams that count.

EVERY DREAM IS A
RELATIONSHIP OPPORTUNITY

In the world of loving relationships, all of our dreams are valid. The largest dreams provide an opportunity for two loving individuals to put their separateness aside, join forces in a dramatic way, and accomplish something that could never be accomplished singlehandedly. When it works—when someone gets the degree they have always desired, the house they have always hoped for, the magical vacation they have fantasized about, the car they so desperately needed—the power of partnership is something to be envied. And the bond is tangibly strengthened.

But the small dreams also provide opportunity—an opportunity for two individuals to learn more about the daily demand for attention, consideration, effective communication, cooperation, and compromise that defines a truly loving partnership. And the emotional payoff for supporting small dreams is often disproportionately large.

"All I Really Want . . ."

When your partner starts a sentence with the words, *"All I really want
. . . ,"* what is your typical reaction? Are you able to hear what he or
she is asking for, even if this request is small? Do you take this
request seriously? Do you start thinking about your own small
dreams? Do you get defensive? Do you tune the whole thing out?
When *you* start a sentence with these four words, how does your
partner respond? And how does it make you feel when your words
fall on deaf ears?

These four words—"All I really want . . ."—are another relationship
gift because they are giving you an opportunity to help your partner
with something that may not be at all obvious to you. And they should
be a signal for you to focus on the request that will follow. It doesn't
matter if someone is asking for an hour of peace and quiet, a clean
kitchen table, an ice cream cone, or a hug. At this special moment,
when these words spill out, this little dream is HUGE. And the partner
who is paying serious attention, and responding to these words seriously, is the partner who is committed to building a stronger team.

Never underestimate the impact of supporting the smallest dreams.

FILL IN THE BLANKS, FILL IN THE DREAMS

Here is a deceptively simple-looking fill-in-the-blank exercise that
has helped jumpstart a lot of couples on the road to "team dreaming."
To begin, copy the following sentence down *six* times on a piece of
paper. Then fill in the blanks. Take as much time as you need, but
don't quit until you have completed all six.

*When my partner says, "All I really want is _____," I
tend to _____. With a little bit of effort, I could
_____ to make that dream come true.*

Let me give you a few examples to help you get started . . .

When my partner says, "All I really want is *a hot shower in the morning,*" I tend to *not pay attention.* With a little bit of effort, I could *spend five minutes less in the shower to ensure that there is some hot water left* to make that dream come true.

When my partner says, "All I really want is *to come home from work just one night and see dinner already on the table,*" I tend to *think to myself, "Me, too!"* With a little bit of effort, I could *give up my daily routine of reading the newspaper before dinner and surprise my partner with a cooked meal one night* to make that dream come true.

When my partner says, "All I really want is *to spend one Christmas Eve without any of your brothers,*" I tend to *say, "But it's my family!"* With a little bit of effort, I could *call my brothers and tell them that the two of us need some time alone this Christmas* to make that dream come true.

When my partner says, "All I really want is *to call a babysitter tonight and go out for a glass of wine,*" I tend to *remind my partner that we don't really have a lot of extra money right now.* With a little bit of effort, I could *save twenty dollars by brown-bagging my lunch for a few days and get on the phone to the babysitter* to make that dream come true.

I realize that this may look like very mundane stuff; it may even look trivial. To your partner, however, it can look like a relationship lifesaver. The dream may be "small," but your actions in support of that dream are sending this very clear, very BIG message: "I hear you, I understand, and I want to help." That is one mighty powerful statement of partnership.

WHAT DOES IT TAKE TO BUILD A GREAT TEAM?

Championship teams are not the teams that only show up for the big games. Championship teams work hard at all the games—practice games, exhibition matches, the works—from the very beginning of the season to the very end. And that is exactly what it's like for a relationship dream team. The strength of a partnership is built through consistent support, fifty-two weeks a year. Supporting big dreams is an act of great love. But standing up for each other's dreams means taking *all* dreams seriously—the biggest dreams, the smallest dreams, and every dream in-between.

SECRET #8:

Tend
the Fire

. ◆ .

At the core of every relationship there is a fire—a source of love, energy, excitement, care, and concern—that is both real and vulnerable. It is the "magic" we feel in our hearts when we are lucky enough to make a true loving connection. And the task of every woman or man who enters a relationship is to watch that fire carefully and respect its fragile nature.

I think that the image of a loving relationship as a live, precious ember that demands constant attention and protection is an image worth holding in the forefront of your consciousness, and preciously close to your heart. The best relationship in the world is not a perpetual motion machine. It will not run forever on great chemistry, good intentions, or the strength of a legal contract. It demands care—an ongoing investment of energy, time, emotion, and attention. There is no automatic pilot. There is no cruise control. You must tend the fire.

THE NEED FOR RENEWAL, THE POWER OF SMALL RITUAL

Love is high-maintenance; it's what makes partnership so different from single life. A regular plan of relationship maintenance is the way ties are continually restored, renewed, and strengthened. Finding rituals within the relationship is a vital way of keeping the embers alive; this is how you can reconnect as a couple time and time again. *Renewal is essential, and ritual is the simplest and most effective path to renewal.*

If a plant needs to be watered every single day and you decide to water it every other day, or once a week, or once in a while, you may be able to keep the plant alive, but it will never be the healthy, full-bodied organism it could be. It's the same for relationships. *Heartfelt connections have to be made constantly and consistently for both partners to feel the strength of their connection.* Otherwise our relationships start to look like neglected plants. And this is where relationship rituals are so valuable.

What Do I Mean by "Relationship Rituals?"

Here are some examples of important relationship rituals: Breakfast. Dinner. Evening walks. Movie night. Sunday morning snuggles. Birthday cards. Anniversary presents. Your annual vacation. There are daily, seasonal, and annual rituals. And all of them are important in their own separate ways because they each contribute a permanent piece to the relationship framework. These are the things you can count on. These are the moments where you feel most visible to your partner and most connected to your partner—intimate, consistent, completely dependable relationship moments. Some of these rituals are so basic or brief that it can be easy to skip them periodically, dismiss them, or neglect them. Yet this is a serious mistake if your goal is a thriving partnership. *Relationship rituals create a baseline that defines your connection, allowing for healthy expectations and an ever-*

increasing sense of trust. Every relationship needs this baseline to function effectively; it's one of the things that most distinguishes the single experience from the coupled experience. Without this baseline, there can be very little real progress in the direction of partnership.

THE DAILY RITUALS

One of the things that surprised me most about married life was the way Jill and I quickly settled into a regular pattern of sitting on the couch together at night, holding hands and watching television. This regular evening ritual is one of the important ways we "tend the fire" and give our connection reinforcement. To an outside observer, a ritual like this may seem unimportant, or even boring. For us, however, it is a vital daily opportunity for reconnection.

Having breakfast together is another common daily ritual that helps a couple tend the fire. With busy schedules and crazy hours, it's often difficult for two people to meet up at the breakfast table on a regular basis; it's so much easier to eat separately or grab breakfast on the run. But even a ten-minute breakfast together is rewarded with a renewed sense of connection. Walking the dog together is yet another potential "fire-tending" daily ritual. The activity *requires* only one person, but when it becomes a regular event for a couple it can add richness to their lives. These are just a few examples. There are many, many more.

Loving connections, no matter how strong they are, require regular reinforcement, and daily rituals provide that reinforcement. The relationship batteries need to be recharged.

"Recharging the relationship batteries"—that's another metaphor that can help you stay focused on building your partnership and keep you from losing sight of opportunities to connect. When we miss those opportunities for dependable connection, the relationship batteries gradually drain. When our behavior is unpredictable, the batteries gradually drain. When we live on automatic pilot and don't slow down enough to make heartfelt connections that register on the "real" meter, the batteries lose energy. Relationship batteries don't die overnight from this kind of neglect, but they do lose their power.

The Real Message of Daily Rituals Is in the Subtext

Daily rituals like the ones I've mentioned don't appear to be terribly complicated. It's the *subtext* that's complicated. *Every time a ritual is honored, coded messages are being sent from partner to partner.* "You are important to me." "I need to spend time with you." "You are my priority." "I miss you when we are apart." "Life feels better when I am sharing it with you." Even if you don't say a single word to each other the entire time, these messages are being constantly broadcast through your commitment to rituals. Take them away, and the relationship suffers.

When a couple takes a few minutes in the morning to have breakfast together, they are not just saying, "Pass the cornflakes." They are also silently saying to each other, "I want us to have these few minutes together before we have to go to work." That's the subtext.

When a couple goes out for their evening walk, they are not just saying, "Isn't it pretty out tonight?" They are also silently saying, "This time we can spend together is more important than anything I could be doing alone." That's the subtext.

When my wife and I are sitting next to each other on the couch, we are not just saying, "Do you want to watch *The West Wing*?" Each of us is saying to the other, "I need this time to reconnect with you. I missed you during the day. And now I need to feel you close by." That's the subtext.

These crucial subtexts need to be communicated through ritual. Words are nice, but words are not always enough. The intention behind those words needs to be supported by actions. The actions give us something to believe in. The actions give us assurance. The actions give us a reason to trust.

GIANT LITTLE RITUALS

Some relationship rituals are so small that they are easily dismissed until their absence creates a problem. *This includes rituals such as . . .*

- the morning greeting.
- the kiss goodbye.
- the "check-in" phone call.
- the evening greeting.
- the kiss goodnight.

Take, for example, the goodbye kiss. There are many times when we leave our partner's side. Sometimes it's when we go to work; sometimes it's to run errands, to see our separate friends, to visit the gym, or to just take a walk.

Each time we separate from our partner for any length of time, we have two choices:

1) *We can acknowledge that separation with a few kind words and, perhaps, a hug and/or kiss, or . . .*
2) *we can just leave.*

Once again, it is in the subtext of each choice where the most valuable information can be found. Every time we leave our partner without acknowledging the separation, the message being sent is: "I'm not really thinking about you right now." That may not be what you are *feeling*, but that's what your behavior says. When you take a moment to share a few words, a hug, or a kiss, your behavior says something very different. More than anything, it says, "I'm not just thinking about *me*."

Let's take out the magnifying glass and look at this little ritual even more closely. There are many variations on the good-bye kiss. There is, for example, the unfocused air kiss, the quick peck, and the sweet kiss that requires a momentary pause. Each of these sends a different message. One says, "Let's get superficial . . . ," one says, "I don't really have time to focus on feelings right now . . . ," and one says, "I'll miss you." Do you know the difference?

Some people might accuse me of splitting hairs here. But most of us, in our bones, really do know the difference between a goodbye kiss that makes us feel visible, important, and loved, and a kiss that doesn't register on the "real" meter and leaves us feeling some kind of void. The latter is an example of something I call a "phantom ritual."

MAKING BIG BREAKTHROUGHS
IN BRIEF MOMENTS

When we are going through the motions but not accessing our feelings, we have fallen into phantom rituals. Ask yourself this question: In that brief moment when I kiss my partner goodbye, am I focused and feeling something in my heart, or have I kicked into automatic pilot? I'm not trying to make a case here for an exhausting morning makeout session; what I'm trying to do is create more awareness around the impact of these daily gestures. *Attending to small rituals isn't just about going through the motions; it's about making those motions count.*

Consider, now, the kiss goodnight, and try to imagine the many different messages this kiss (or its absence) can convey. Does your goodnight kiss say to your partner, "I hope you sleep well, and I can't wait to see you again in the morning." Or is it saying something like, "I'm too tired to think about you right now . . ." or "I'm feeling very single right now . . ." or "Adios, stranger." In other words, is it a kiss or a kiss-off? It doesn't take a lot of work to give this evening ritual constructive meaning. All that is required is a moment of your time when you are willing to pause—to stop whatever it is that you are doing (reading, working, listening to music through headphones, worrying about the next day) and acknowledge the fact that someone is going to sleep. We're not talking about a major production here; this can be accomplished lovingly in fifteen seconds.

And what about your morning greeting? This simple daily ritual has the potential to give your relationship a little bit of new strength and life every day, or to chip away at that strength and life. This is your decision to make every single morning. How do you treat your partner when you see each other for the very first time that day? Do you give your partner a big smile, a gentle hug, or a kiss that says, "I'm so happy to see you." Or does your behavior send a very different kind of message—a message like, "Oh, it's you again . . ." or "I already have too much on my mind to focus on you . . ." or "You need to stay away from me until I've had my coffee."

I have a friend who gets up two hours earlier than his wife every morning because he has a long commute to his office. His wife insists that he wake her up each morning for just one minute so that she can see him, and give him a quick but sincere hug before he leaves the house. Sometimes she can't fall back to sleep right away, but she's willing to lose those few minutes because she is completely clear how much comfort this little ritual gives them both, and how this comfort carries through the day.

SMALL RITUALS ACKNOWLEDGE THE DIFFICULTY OF SEPARATION

There is another reason it's so important to attend to daily separations with some heartfelt ritual: Separation is *hard*! Every time we say goodbye—whether we're going to work, going to the other side of town, or going to sleep for the night—we feel a little tear in the fabric of our connection. Ritual is how we mend that tear; it's a daily practice of tying tiny but vital knots.

Many men and women have become numb to the discomfort of separation; they have long since filled in that discomfort with food, or cigarettes, or some busy behavior. Part of building a healthier partnership is reconnecting to the discomfort of disconnecting. I'm not trying to be funny here. Sometimes, it is important to feel the anxiety or melancholy that comes from hours of separation. It keeps us human. It reminds us of how much our partners mean to us. It reminds us that we have made a bond in the chambers of our heart. And it keeps us aware of our need to constantly attend to daily opportunities for reconnection.

I'm not suggesting that you need to be in agony every morning when you head to your office, or every evening when you drift off to sleep. But I *am* suggesting that separation—even when it's just for a matter of hours—is harder than most of us are willing to admit. And the salve for our discomfort is small, loving rituals.

Checking in to Say "I'm Thinking About You"

Some of us have regular opportunities to see our partner throughout the day, a luxury afforded to us by the nature of our work and lifestyle. But the majority of men and women have to live through the daily experience of lengthy separations that are dictated by the demands of our complex lives. When a hard day's work, or hard day's play, takes you and your partner to different corners of the neighborhood, the city, or the state, how do you attend to that unavoidable separation? The answer is this: the "check-in" ritual.

When the demands of work and/or family start to consume you, it's terribly easy to lose track of time. The hours pass in a blur, and the day is often over before you know it. That's the daily check-*out*, and I understand how easily that happens. But each time we let that day pass without making some attempt to reach out to our partner, we are depriving our partner of a valuable gift—the gift of reassurance. Your partner needs to know that he/she is in your thoughts during these separations. And the only way to convey that warm and loving inner experience is to act on it before the day goes by.

I know couples who phone each other at least once a day, I know couples who e-mail each other at least once a day (and many who e-mail each other constantly), and I know couples who manage to meet for coffee. But every couple I know who prioritizes partnership is committed to this daily check-in ritual. Can your relationship survive without it? Probably. But why should it have to? Especially when it takes so little effort to give your connection the extra layer of loving feeling by this simple ritual.

The check-in is another one of those giant little rituals that delivers its most powerful message in the subtext. Whether you use these few moments to talk about work, the weather, or what you want for dinner, one message you are always sending is this: "You may be out of sight, but you are not out of mind." Another message is: "Even though we're apart, I never feel single." No matter how much we love and trust our partners, these are two messages we never get tired of hearing.

The Homecoming Ritual

Last year, after giving a brief talk at a local bookstore about relationships and "commitmentphobia," I was approached by the manager who wanted to share something personal with me about his marriage. "My wife and I have been married for almost five years," he began, "and I'd like to think that we're very happy together. Yet I must confess that I'm so tired at the end of every day that I can't wait to get home, open a book, and tune the world out. While I'm always happy to see my wife at the end of the day, I don't make reconnecting a priority. I always thought this was something my wife 'accepted' and 'understood,' but now I'm not so sure."

This man's unusual candor has stayed with me, and it's one of the reasons I knew that I had to highlight the importance of the ritual I call "the homecoming." Think about this: How do you greet your partner at the end of the day? What words or gestures do you offer to welcome your mate back into your world? Do you stop, focus, and make these words and gestures meaningful? Or is your homecoming curt, without sincerity, without feeling, or practically nonexistent?

Here are some typical homecoming scenarios that leave a partner feeling invisible, unimportant, or disconnected.

◆ *Rafael can't wait to get to his computer and go on-line the minute he walks in the door at the end of the day. By the time his wife Marla gets home from her job, Rafael is already lost in the World Wide Web. He may greet Marla with a few words, but he almost never looks up from his screen.*

◆ *When Jenny walks in the door, she makes a beeline for her answering machine. By the time her partner Warren gets home, Jenny is usually engrossed in a phone conversation with one of her girlfriends or with her mother. She nods to Warren when he walks in the door, but rarely interrupts her phone conversation.*

◆ *Abe gets home very late from work three nights a week and is always famished. On most of these late nights he stops in the kitchen and spends five or ten minutes finding something to munch on before he looks for his wife.*

A Sixty-Second Solution
That Heals Daily Separations

When we know that our partner is going to walk through that front door every evening without fail (or be on the other side of that door waiting when we walk through it), it's easy to take their dependability for granted. Instead of investing our energy in a meaningful ritual of reconnection, we get lost in personal rituals or old rituals from our single days, like watching TV, chatting on the phone, reading the paper, or surfing the net. But these other rituals can easily turn into rituals of *disconnection* when we don't put our partnership first.

Daily separations need to be followed by an acknowledgment that the separation is over; the moment of "rejoining" needs to be marked. This homecoming ritual, like the other small rituals I've been talking about, doesn't have to be a lavish, time-consuming production. But it has to be done in a way that makes it count. This can be done with a loving smile, a few thoughtful words, or a sincere hug or kiss. But a loving message needs to be sent from partner to partner—a message that somehow says, "I'm happy to see you." This is an important example of what it means to not act "single."

Maybe you're thinking to yourself, "I'm *always* happy to see my partner at the end of the day." But my question is this: Does your behavior bring that message across *clearly* every day? When your head is buried in a book or a newspaper, your partner doesn't always know that you're happy to see him/her. When your eyes are glued to a screen or monitor, your partner doesn't always realize that you're happy to see him/her. When your ear is pressed to the phone and you can barely manage a nod in your partner's direction, your partner doesn't always know that you are happy to see him/her. When you are listening to music through headphones and you can barely hear your partner's words, how can your partner know that you are happy to see him/her? Your partner is looking for cues in your eye contact, your tone of voice, and your body language. If your focus is somewhere else, your partner *feels* that your focus is somewhere else, and this makes it hard to feel *welcome*.

When you or your partner walk through that door at the end of the day, it's so important to be aware of the very simple, but powerful messages you are broadcasting to the person you love.

Think about your subtle messages:

- *Think about the message your eyes are giving.* Are you making genuine eye contact? Do you hold your partner's gaze?
- *Think about the message your words are giving.* Do your words convey warmth and a sense of welcome?

- *Think about the message your body is giving.* Do you stop whatever you are doing and offer a heartfelt hug and/or kiss?
- *Think about the message your actions are giving.* Do you put down, turn off, or turn away from whatever it is you are doing and turn your attention to your partner, even if it is only for a minute?

One minute—maybe even less. That's all that is required— then you can go back to your book, your magazine, your computer, or whatever. But in that minute you set the tone for the evening. And with each week and month of these one-minute relationship moments, you help set the tone for the entire relationship. The impact, whether it is positive or negative, is cumulative. So make that minute count.

CELEBRATING HOLIDAYS, BIRTHDAYS, AND OTHER IMPORTANT DAYS

◆ *Silvio's favorite holiday ritual is driving around the suburbs of Minneapolis two weeks before Christmas Day with his partner Shana and looking for the perfect tree.*

◆ *Petra knows that when she wakes up on the morning of her birthday there will be cards, confetti, and a piece of chocolate waiting for her at the breakfast table, magically placed there every year by "the birthday fairy" (i.e., her partner Gil).*

◆ *What Cassie loves most about the summer is taking the train to Coney Island every Sunday with her husband, walking the boardwalk, and eating hot dogs and french fries.*

◆ *Every year at Passover, Denise labors to recreate the onion pancakes that her husband's grandmother made for him when he was a small child.*

For some people, a birthday is just a birthday, a weekend is just a weekend, and a holiday is just something to "get through." These annual, seasonal, or regular events can easily become a chore, a nuisance, or a relationship ghost that doesn't even show up on the radar. But, as these scenarios so clearly demonstrate, we can create magical feelings in our partnerships by committing ourselves to recognize, honor, and celebrate the important days and times in our lives.

Holidays, birthdays, and other special days and times of the year are designed for ritual embellishments. They are easy to remember—usually being clearly marked by the seasons, the calendars, the store windows, and the closing of our office doors. Yet it still takes energy and effort to take these moments and transform them into connective relationship tissue.

Are you making the most out of these opportunities for loving ritual? Do you give your partner—and yourself—something to look forward to? Is your behavior consistent, so your partner can build expectations without risking disappointment? *Consistency* is the key here. *Elaborate celebrations are certainly nice, but it is only the consistent ritual that has the strength and stability to be a partnership building block.*

"We Need a Vacation!"

When was the last time you and your partner took a few days together away from the distractions of work, household chores and worries, friends and family? The concept of vacation time is shrinking in this country. People who used to try and "steal a few weeks" are now struggling to steal a few days or even a few hours. Some of us have given up all hope of taking a vacation away from home. We may cart laptops and cell phones and pagers with us wherever we go to because we don't trust the stability of our clients, our bosses, the stock market, and our latest business deal. And, in the process, we keep disconnecting from the one person whose stability we trust.

Vacations continue to be one of the most healing, grounding, and rejuvenating relationship rituals. Couples rediscover their sex lives. They rediscover their capacity for simple pleasures. They rediscover their healthy priorities. They rediscover how much more loving and connected they can feel when everyone has had enough sleep. They rediscover their "other half." And they rediscover their reasons for being in a partnership. Do you know any couple that *doesn't* need this?

A lot of people think they can get away with skipping or abbreviating their vacations. Many think they can turn their vacation time into work time and not pay a price. But experience tells me that this thinking is terribly naive. ***If you are part of a couple, your relationship depends on a consistent schedule of renewal to counter the many forces that leave us feeling separate and alone.*** Vacations—*real* vacations where jobs and other distractions have to sit in the back seat—are an ideal opportunity for that renewal.

And what about the kids? Some couples wouldn't dream of going on vacation without their children, while others can't wait to drop the kids off at grandma's house. Is one choice any healthier than the other? Not necessarily. While I realize that there are some couples that desperately need to have more time alone (and I encourage these couples to make that time *now*), I also know that family vacations can be an equally loving experience that connects the family and builds wonderful memories. But even in the context of a family vacation, I encourage the adults to have some private time and establish healthy boundaries with the children—and to defend those boundaries. The truth is that all vacations have the potential to renew love and connection if your focus is on personal relationships.

The Importance of Anniversary

Louis and Cassie, two of my closest friends, have been married almost twenty years, and I often look to their relationship as a role model for my own. Every year, for those past twenty years, Louis and Cassie have celebrated *three* wedding anniversaries. They celebrate the day they got married in San Francisco, the day they got married *again* in New York City for the friends and relatives who could not travel to the west coast, and the day they exchanged their vows during a trip to Europe the first year they were married. Years ago, when I knew precious little about partnership, and was more cynical than I care to admit, I would often tease Louis and Cassie about their many anniversaries. But when I met Jill, I got a very fast education about the importance of anniversaries, and the teasing stopped.

The celebration of anniversaries is a vital relationship ritual because it is your bridge from the past to the future. But this bridge only gets built if you approach the ritual with sincerity.

Are you sending the right anniversary message?

- If you are always forgetting important days, you are not sending a loving message.
- If your personal assistant is the one who orders the flowers or buys the presents for your partner, you are losing the opportunity to feel genuinely connected.
- If you always wait till the absolute last minute to rush out and grab whatever card or gift you can quickly find, you are cheating yourself of the opportunity to feel the weight of the event.
- If you use extravagance as a substitute for thoughtfulness, you are missing the meaning of the ritual.
- If you're not willing to stop and take time from your day to be with your partner and acknowledge the importance of the anniversary, both of you are being deprived of the unique opportunity to strengthen your bond.

Making Those Anniversaries Count

It can be very easy to forget an anniversary. Most of us have such busy lives, working so hard and running so fast, that special days creep up on us before we even notice. But when those days arrive, you have to stop. Think of it as part of your relationship job description: *Stop and celebrate important anniversaries.* Because every time you set aside a day, or even an hour, to mark the day, you are taking another giant step in the direction of permanent partnership.

Here are four anniversary recommendations that can help keep your relationship vital . . .

1) *Don't limit yourself to one anniversary.* There's nothing wrong with having more than one. Find reasons to celebrate your connection.
2) *Plan ahead.* Don't stumble onto the day unprepared. Let your preparation reinforce your connection.
3) *Take responsibility.* This is *your* anniversary—don't dilute its meaning by enlisting other people to do your shopping, your planning, or your thinking.
4) *Take time out.* Stop whatever you normally do (for an hour, for an afternoon, or for a long weekend) and give yourself and your partner a chance to feel the specialness of the event.

Many people will try to argue that it's far more important to be a consistently loving partner every day of the year than it is to be a good anniversary partner once or twice a year. While I know this is true, I also know that this truth does not diminish the power or the importance of the anniversary ritual. This ritual is an integral part of your relationship framework, and you want that framework to be loving.

LOVING REMINDERS: USING THE PAST TO CELEBRATE THE PRESENT

I have discovered, in the past few years, that one of the most wonderful things about celebrating an anniversary is the opportunity it provides to revisit the original day. For Jill and I, each anniversary is a chance to remind ourselves what it is, exactly, that we are celebrating.

When we celebrate the anniversary of our first date, for example, we exchange stories about our memories of that day. Jill talks about how badly her stomach ached for the first hour, and how upset she was that she burned the barbecued chicken. I talk about how nervous I was driving across the city to get to her house (I was certain that my car would break down), and how thrilled I was to be eating one of my favorite foods: burned barbecue chicken. Sometimes these memories make us laugh, sometimes they make us teary, and sometimes they get us into an argument over whose version is the real version. But they always leave us feeling especially close.

Loving reminders are an important way to reinforce the experience of an anniversary, or *any* day, and they are a vital piece of the ritual experience. Reaching back into the past breathes new life into that past, while adding a layer of richness to the present. Memories are more vibrant. Nostalgia is intensified. And the bond gains strength. I know couples who recreate their first date once a year, going back to the same restaurant and even ordering the same food. I know couples who, at least once a year, travel great distances to revisit the place where they first met. I know couples who sit down every single year to watch videos of their engagement party, wedding ceremony, and honeymoon. And I know couples who write down their special relationship memories on anniversaries, birthdays, or New Year's Eve and exchange these unusual love letters.

Any special relationship moment can be revisited, or even recreated as a reminder of why you love each other and why you're together. When we neglect or forget the past, we lose some of the details that make our partnership so special. Using loving reminders as a relationship ritual may require a little effort at times, but that effort has both immediate and long-term rewards.

REMEMBERING THE MORE DIFFICULT MOMENTS: ANOTHER POWERFUL RITUAL

Tending the fire is a process that isn't limited to the celebration of good moments and good memories. Tending the fire also requires us to respect, honor, and make efforts to connect around challenging moments and challenging memories.

Every man and every woman has had to endure loss in their lifetimes. Some of us have lost not just grandparents, but parents, siblings, aunts, uncles, cousins, or dear friends. Some of us have lost loving partners. Many of us have lost pets. And all of these losses stay with us somewhere in the psyche, and revisit us throughout our lives. Other difficult times and difficult facts of life also have a way of hanging around the psyche and revisiting on occasion—the time you had a big fight with your partner, the time you lost your job, the time your house got robbed, the time you got seriously depressed.

It's only human to want to avoid your own painful memories, and to wish you could hide from your partner's unpleasant memories until they pass. But the emotional "anniversaries" of challenging times are really a chance for partners to feel each other's love and support in the deepest and most lasting ways.

I know many men and women who go with their partners on regular trips to family gravesites. I know men and women who regularly accompany their partners on custody visitations. I know one woman who goes with her husband once every two weeks to visit his broth-

er in a long-term care facility. And I even know a couple that celebrates the anniversary of their worst fight. These rituals may be difficult, or awkward; but they are also a celebration of partnership, and
they give the relationship more muscle.

CREATING NEW RITUALS
TO TEND THE FIRE

Smart couples are always looking for new rituals to reinforce and
expand their sense of partnership. Perhaps this means going to the
gym together every Saturday (instead of always working out separately
at different times and on different days), going for a leisurely walk
together one or two nights a week (instead of always splintering off
into separate evening activities), finding a vacation spot you return to
regularly, finding a place of worship that meets everyone's spiritual
needs, doing something charitable together once a month, or making
every Monday night "movie night." The options are unlimited. You just
need to get started. Here are a few rules of thumb to help.

How to Create Effective New Rituals

• *Think Small.*

Make the "giant little rituals"—the daily greetings, the regular
check-ins, etc.—your very first priority. Are these rituals cemented
into your daily routine? These are the basics, and where you need to
begin. Don't, for example, make the very common mistake of being
the kind of person who is always buying his or her partner cute cards
and gifts, but also rushing out the door every morning without giving
their partner a thoughtful "goodbye." The "new" rituals you need
most in your relationship may be the small, fundamental ones you
have been neglecting all along.

- *Think simple.*

Elaborate rituals (expensive and/or time-consuming) are certainly exciting, but they are hard to keep up. Elaborate rituals also have the potential to eclipse smaller, more dependable rituals. If, for example, you are sacrificing the weekly romantic dinner-dates that provide regular dollops of partnership glue for your once-a-year trip to Paris, you may be losing more than you gain.

- *Think long-term.*

Twice-in-a-lifetime extravaganzas don't have the same weight as things you can return to again and again, month after month and year after year. Ask yourself this: Does this ritual have a long future we can both work on and count on? The most effective rituals are the ones you can look back on with nostalgia and look forward to with anticipation at the very same time. Don't focus on creating memorable experiences—focus on creating *consistent* experiences with a solid future.

- *Think personal.*

Look for rituals that are custom-made for *your* partnership. Rituals that had a lot of meaning for you in past relationships may not have the same meaning for your current partner (or you). And some rituals work a lot better in the movies or on TV than they do in real life. It can be very romantic, to give one example, to go for long drives in the countryside every weekend—but not if your partner has miserable seasonal allergies.

- *Think about hearts.*

Not every partnership ritual feeds the heart—some are just patterns that are convenient, or hard to break. Fighting is a ritual in some partnerships, but it's certainly not a pleasurable one. Going to visit relatives every week is a ritual, but it's not a particularly constructive one if family issues are a source of constant conflict. Getting smashed on martinis every Friday night is another ritual, but it's damaging to our hearts and livers. As you think about creating new rituals, use your heart to feel your way through your options. Look for rituals that will leave both partners with a sense of bonding and renewal.

• *Think about commitment.*

The power of ritual rests in your personal commitment—this is the special ingredient that gives it credibility and strength. Don't be whimsical about your choices or your plans. Don't head in new directions that you know, right from the start, you won't pursue consistently. Make it a priority to minimize disappointment—constant let-downs create bad feelings between partners. Focus on rituals where you know you can honor your commitment.

SECRET #9:

Allow for Separateness

· ◆ ·

Isaac and Allison have an ongoing argument that never manages to get resolved. It's an argument about separateness.

Isaac and Allison work together six days a week in a small photocopy shop that they bought seven years ago. They both work very hard, and at the end of a long day, they both need to relax. Not surprisingly, they have very two different ideas about what it means to relax. Allison would absolutely love to go out with friends—this is her favorite way to unwind. Isaac, on the other hand, likes nothing more than sitting quietly at home and reading a great "escapist" novel. And this is where the problems start.

Isaac hates spending his evenings with groups of people. He's willing to go with Allison to a restaurant, to a movie, to a concert—anything that's just the two of them together, by themselves.

Allison is reluctant to socialize without Isaac. And Isaac doesn't support that solution, either. It makes him angry, and probably at least a little bit jealous. Both Isaac and Allison believe that in the best of all possible worlds, a couple should always be at each other's side.

However, when Allison *is* at Isaac's side in the evening, she has another problem. As soon as Isaac picks up a book and starts reading, Allison feels lonely. She wants to be doing something *together*—even if that "something" is just watching television. She wants to share *every* experience, and she hates the way Isaac can become engrossed in his own individual experience of reading. She thinks it's selfish and mean.

Most of the time Isaac and Allison manage to contain their feelings about these differences, but every now and then they start to bicker. And they aren't afraid to bicker in loud voices right in front of their customers. If you're one of their regular customers, you've probably heard them argue too many times; it amazes some people that Isaac and Allison are still together. By the time I finished interviewing Isaac and Allison, I too was amazed. I have never felt so tense in the presence of two people who insist they have a good relationship.

WHEN YOU SQUEEZE TOO TIGHT, NO ONE CAN BREATHE

We all know people who are like Isaac and Allison. For example:

♦ *Martha won't go to her mother's house without her husband, Doug, even though her mother and Doug always fight, and nobody has a nice time.*

♦ *Fredda absolutely insists that her husband drive her every place she goes even though she has a perfectly valid driver's license.*

♦ *Josie won't let her boyfriend, Frank, spend time with any of his male friends unless she's there, which makes him not want to spend time with them because the situation becomes too strained.*

◆ *Bill can't spend more than thirty minutes with friends without becoming anxious and looking for a telephone so he can call his girlfriend Sandra.*

These are all good examples of *fragile* partnerships—fragile because one or both partners are holding on too tight, making it difficult for the relationship to "breathe." Here is one more relationship fact: Truly loving couples know the difference between *partnership* and *fusion.* They sacrifice and labor to accomplish the first, and run like hell from the second. The distinction is crucial. And the lack of distinction takes its toll on a relationship, as you can see from the example of Isaac and Allison. To create a lasting, effective partnership, you have to allow for separateness.

HEALTHY SEPARATENESS GIVES A RELATIONSHIP STRENGTH

For the past eight chapters I have examined, often in minute detail, the art of "joining" and connecting to create a greater sense of partnership. So it may seem a little bit strange that in this final chapter I'm suddenly talking about the need for separateness. It's very hard for some people to comprehend the value of separateness in a loving relationship—particularly because it can be so *scary.* I know that of all the "love secrets," this has certainly been the most difficult one for *me* to actively practice. Yet I also know that in the best relationships, both partners understand, respect, and support the ongoing need for a healthy experience of separateness.

A relationship can't work if either partner is trying to crush the other's individual spirit. The growth of a strong relationship depends, in part, on the continued growth of the individuals involved—individual spirit is a magical ingredient in the recipe for a loving relationship. And this recipe never changes. Let's be very clear here: This is not about celebrating disconnection. This is about acknowledging, supporting, and (dare I say it?) *enjoying* healthy differences—different needs, different interests, different schedules, different tastes, different friends, different passions, different temperaments, different priorities, different experiences, different feelings—in the pursuit of love and growth. These differences give a relationship its strength and richness; fear of these differences makes a relationship fragile.

Letting Go of a Powerful Relationship Fantasy

"Healthy separateness" is an easier thing to preach than it is to practice, and there are many reasons why this is true. The very first obstacle to healthy separateness is something most of us have had in our possession long before we ever had the good fortune to find a loving partner. That obstacle is our fantasy definition of "togetherness."

By the time you find a potential partnership, chances are you have spent many years consciously, and unconsciously, refining your picture of an ideal partnership. And, if you're anything like me, the thing that gives your picture its warmth and fuzziness is the togetherness. Sure, you've dreamed about passion, about sex, about romantic moments, and maybe even about having children and raising a family. But the images most of us cling to are the images of *being* with someone—eating together, sleeping together, playing together, relaxing together, cuddling together, traveling together, maybe even working together. Together is the operative word here—as in, "*never alone again*"—and it's something most of us have thought about a lot during the many days, weeks, months, and years that we've been alone. What we have *not* thought about in our relationship fantasies is being *separate*. That thought is a luxury that only a good relationship can provide.

Here's the problem: These very old, very comforting togetherness fantasies can create a lot of confusion, disappointment, and frustration when a real partner shows up. Why? Because you and your partner are likely to have very different fantasies of togetherness, and very different needs for separateness. This doesn't mean something is wrong; it only means that you have found something real. And your ability to put aside your togetherness fantasies and adjust to the "sometimes together, sometimes not" reality of your unique partnership is going to go a long way toward scripting your success.

Togetherness is certainly one of the most wonderful aspects of partnership. There's no denying it. And when your connection is strong and healthy, togetherness is something you will always feel in your heart. But, practically speaking, separation and separateness are unavoidable aspects of partnership. This may not be your fantasy, but it *must* be part of your reality if your reality is going to last.

What Happened to That Perfect Beginning?

When a relationship is in its infancy, it often feels as though there will never be a single moment when you and the one you love will enjoy being apart—never a single moment when you will *want* to be apart. This is not a relationship fantasy; it is a relationship reality that is often referred to as "the pink period." Most relationships enjoy this very special pink period. But it does not last forever, and it is not supposed to.

As trust and intimacy grow, both partners typically begin to feel as though they would like to do at least a few things separately. This is part of a healthy evolution of a couple; it's a stage that tells you that the relationship is safe and can be counted on. I call it *"the stage of healthy separation."* When you go to work in the morning, you expect your home to be there when you return. It's solid. The same thing is true of a partnership in which a solid sense of fundamental connection has been made.

Yet the sudden appearance of a desire for separateness sends many people into a panic. "Why am I having these feelings?" we ask ourselves. "Have I fallen out of love? Is something wrong? Is it the beginning of the end?" "Why is my partner having these feelings?" we also ask ourselves. "Have I done something wrong? Is my partner cheating? Is my partner having a commitment crisis?"

This crucial second stage in the relationship—the stage of healthy separation—is a pivotal one in the development of a partnership. When we appreciate it and welcome it, we are saying to our partner, "Our bond is strong enough for us to still be individuals within this partnership." But when we panic and start to cling, try to be controlling, or act out in destructrive ways, we send a very different message: "I can't tolerate separateness."

Wanting to Be "Of One Mind," Wanting to Be "Of One Heart"

These are two more fantasy variations on the theme of togetherness that often get in the way of successful partnership. In the world of romantic fiction, exquisite merger is the ideal. And, as I already mentioned in the first chapter, it isn't unusual to feel an overwhelming sense of fusion at the height of the earliest, most romantic phase of relationship development. But in the day-to-day experience of an ongoing serious partnership, that ideal quickly gives way to a reality that doesn't always have the same sense of enchantment. Some of us question this transition—we wonder if we have fallen out of love, if we've made a bad choice, or if we've done something to make our partner act more distant. Yet whether we like this transition or not, it's actually a good thing.

In real life, hearts touch, but they don't fuse into one organ with only one set of feelings. Minds connect, but they don't melt into one set of thoughts. Early in a relationship, the feelings of union can be very powerful, and it's not unusual to feel bonded like two halves of a popsicle. But when I meet long-established couples who are still acting as though they are two halves of the same popsicle, I get very nervous. I get nervous because I know that this merged behavior is rarely prompted by a perfect union. Far more often, it is driven by a fear of being different, a fear of being rejected, and a fear of being alone. "Two hearts that beat as one" is a better premise for a sci-fi film than it is for a loving relationship; I have said this many times. And would you really want to be so like-minded that your partner knows your every thought? To me, that sounds pretty scary.

GETTING SERIOUS
ABOUT BEING SEPARATE

There are many reasons why separateness can be so difficult for some people. We already talked about one reason: powerful togetherness fantasies that don't mesh with partnership realities. *Here are some other reasons why separateness can be tough:*

- Fear of abandonment
- Jealousy, insecurity, and low self-esteem
- Antiquated role models
- Inappropriate boundaries
- Painful relationship history

Though it's easy for us to not take some of these issues so seriously, every one of them can have a tremendous impact on a developing partnership. I think it's important to take the time here to look at each of them in greater detail.

Taking Your Fear of Abandonment Seriously

Asa likes to think of himself as an emotionally strong, healthy partner. When he and his girlfriend Carmen are together, he's a pillar of strength for her. Yet when Carmen goes away once a month to visit her sick mother, Asa quickly starts to feel like a helpless infant. He loses interest in his work. He loses interest in his hobbies. And he anxiously awaits every phone call from Carmen. Essentially, Asa's life comes to a halt, and it doesn't start back up until Carmen returns. Carmen needs Asa's support when she's with her mother—it's an emotional drain for her. Yet every time they speak on the phone, Asa sounds distant and angry.

When Asa was two years old, his mother was hospitalized for almost four weeks. What is hard for Asa to understand is that every time Carmen goes away for more than a day, the agony of his childhood abandonment is being relived. These periods of feeling helpless are incredibly painful for Asa, and he often wonders whether or not he can stay in a relationship with a partner who has to travel on a regular basis.

I have heard hundreds of versions of this story, and I must confess that I have my own unpleasant version. I fully understand the impact of childhood abandonment—both physical and emotional abandonment—on our capacity to tolerate separateness as adults. This is serious stuff.

Asa has never been to a therapist or a counselor, and he has never given much thought to the impact of his early history. But this history is controlling his ability to survive in a *loving* relationship. Asa needs to take his fear of abandonment more seriously. It doesn't matter how strong he is when he and Carmen are together—their separations reveal his vulnerability. If he wants his partnership to flourish, he needs to find some help. And, in the meantime, he and Carmen need to establish *predictable* ways of staying connected (telephone, e-mail, etc.) during their separations.

When the anticipation of separation creates anxiety or anger, when separateness feels like punishment, and when time alone always feels like a "time out," the easiest thing to do is to blame our partners. We hurl accusations such as, "You were away too long!" "You're not talking to me!" or "If you loved me you'd want to be with me!" Our feelings are so real, and often so painful, we want our partners to know how much we suffer. We also want them to know that they have the power to make us feel better. But all of this masks the core issue: a vulnerability that has been shaped by our own history of abandonment. Your partner can work with you to heal some of these injuries, but healing doesn't start until you take responsibility for your own fears. *Allowing for separateness means learning to manage your separation anxiety.*

Dealing With Jealousy, Insecurity, and Low Self-Esteem

Howard and Donna have been together as a couple for almost four years, yet Howard is still uncomfortable with Donna's independent spirit. When Donna tells Howard she needs a few hours to just be by herself, Howard knows that she is being completely clear and forthright, and he knows that Donna is very much in love with him. Yet he still has jealous fantasies that Donna may be spending this time with another man.

Howard rarely feels the need for the "alone time" that Donna needs, and this frustrates him. This morning Howard fell into a bad relationship trap of his own creation. Feeling uncomfortable with his own jealous tendencies, he tried to stir some jealousy in Donna by announcing that he was thinking about going to New York City by himself for two days to attend the Jazz Festival. Donna's reaction was a very sincere and supportive, "That sounds great honey . . . you'd love that!" Now Howard is feeling even more frustrated, more angry, and more suspicious. He doesn't want to spend two days in New York City by himself. He wanted Donna to protest. Why doesn't Donna get jealous the way he does? How can anyone be that secure?

The jealousy and insecurity that stem from low self-esteem can make every difference between partners unpleasant, and every separation uncomfortable. This makes it hard to allow for healthy separateness. And the problem doesn't end there. This continual discomfort often leads to bad relationship decisions and destructive behavior. We agree when we want to disagree, we stay when we want to go, we say yes when we want to say no—all because we're afraid to rock the relationship boat and magnify our feelings of separateness. But trying to control and protect a partnership this way only, as I said earlier, makes the relationship more fragile.

In our fantasies most of us imagine that being in a loving relationship would bolster our self-esteem and dismantle our jealousies and insecurities. And this is certainly possible. Yet for some men and women, being in a loving relationship triggers anxieties that create the opposite effect: we may sometimes feel *more* vulnerable and *more* insecure because we have so much more to lose. The love of a good partner can go a long way toward healing the injuries that lead to low self-esteem, but that love is not a substitute for the necessary experience of self-love. Sometimes being a better partner means taking better care of yourself.

Installing New Role-Model Software

♦ *Arnie grew up in a household where his mother and father were always together. They ran a business together; they played competitive bridge together three nights a week; they had no close friends other than each other. When Arnie's wife leaves for three hours every Saturday morning to do her volunteer work as a Big Sister, Arnie feels angry and unhappy.*

♦ *Benjamin grew up in a household where the entire family always sat down for dinner together at 6:30 P.M. Every time his fiancée comes home from work and says, "I had a really big lunch today— you're on your own for dinner," he feels that something is wrong with the relationship.*

Arnie and Benjamin have loving relationships that most men and women would envy, yet they are both unhappy because some old piece of relationship software in their brains is telling them to be unhappy. Old programs are very powerful. They also make relationships simpler, in some ways, because they don't ask us to carve out a new and unique partnership with its own rules. But when that old software keeps sending up "error messages" it may be a sign that

Allow for Separateness

something is wrong with the *program*, not the relationship.

Consider some of the other old "fusion" programs that may be rattling around in your brain right now. What are some of the *musts* you haven't quite let go of? Does being in a successful relationship require that you and your partner share all of the same interests? Keep the same schedule? Have the same friends? Eat the same foods? Like the same movies? Drive the same car? Wear outfits that match? Now ask yourself this: Do you view every difference as a personal failure?

Are there other relationship "rules" that keep you fused? Do you believe, for example, that "When we're at a party we can't leave each other's side" or "We always have to present a united front to the world" or "Separate vacations are unacceptable" or "There is no such thing as too much togetherness?" In other words, is there any room in your world for healthy separateness?

Healthy separation is a vital part of any relationship software that will be viable in the new millenium. Relationship models that you have adopted from your past may have worked many years ago when partnership was more tightly scripted, but very few are Y2K compliant. You can make yourself miserable yearning for the "good old days," or you can upgrade your attitudes and appreciate the potential richness of a more complex partnership.

Learning to Draw The Line

◆ *Jenna has insinuated herself into every friendship her fiancé Mitch has, and she is always incorporating herself into Mitch's plans. Contrast this with Anna, who is always encouraging her boyfriend Rudy to take private time to cultivate his important friendships.*

◆ *Harry often listens in on his wife's telephone conversations. He doesn't believe there should be any boundaries in their relationship. Contrast this with Sofia, who always excuses herself and leaves the room when her husband gets a personal phone call.*

213

◆ *Bernard makes every decision about his partner Ellen's car—when to service it, when to fix it, who to bring it to, etc. Most of these decisions are good decisions, but it doesn't really matter. Ellen is furious that she never gets the chance to decide for herself—even if that means making a mistake. How else will she ever learn?*

Being in a relationship does not require surrendering your own separateness. You are not supposed to surrender your soul. You are still entitled, for example, to have your own friends (even if your partner doesn't like them), to make your own plans (even if your partner isn't interested), to have private time (even if your partner doesn't need that), to have your own thoughts and feelings (even if your partner has different thoughts and feelings), and to make some decisions on your own.

Some of us need to strengthen our ability to draw healthy boundaries. And if you grew up in a household where boundaries were not clear, this is a challenging task. Start by practicing expressions of individuality such as, "I need to do this myself," "I need to be alone for a few minutes," "I don't really agree," "I'm not in the mood to share tonight," and "I'm not really in the mood for pizza . . . I'm going to make myself a hamburger." Also try to shore up some healthy boundaries with the help of these five "healthy separateness mantras":

Mantras for Healthy Separateness

- "I am entitled some personal space, and so is my partner."
- "To hover is to smother."
- "My independent spirit enhances our relationship."
- "Partnership is not fusion."
- "There *is* such a thing as "too much togetherness""

I have said this many times, but I am going to say it once more: In a loving, effective partnership, individuality is a *good* thing.

214

Rewriting a Painful History

- *Every time Rhoda's husband calls from work to say that he's running a little bit late, Rhoda can't help thinking about the first husband she divorced because he had an affair with his secretary.*
- *Every time Ally picks up a book and starts reading, her boyfriend Jason can't help thinking about his ex-girlfriend who was always busy with something that didn't involve him.*
- *Every time Otis goes to a basketball game without Penny, she can't help thinking about her ex-husband who nearly bankrupted them with his secret gambling addiction.*

Sometimes our discomfort with separateness is a clear product of our romantic disappointments and disasters. Let's face it—very few of us have sailed smoothly through the world of love and romance. Some of us have been lied to. Some of us have been cheated on. Some of us have been taken for granted. And we've all been rejected.

Clinging to your history makes you cling to your partner. It's hard to allow for separateness when separateness has brought you anguish. But how do you break free from that history so that both you and your partner can enjoy a *healthy*—i.e., positive, loving, mutually gratifying—experience of separateness? Wounds take time to close, but they do close when they are carefully attended to. Part of the healing process necessitates risk—that's something you can't avoid. But another important part of the healing process is a more concious acknowledgment of your past. Being able to talk about your history and your fears to your partner, or to a therapist, helps diminish their power.

YOUR PARTNER IS NOT YOUR MIRROR IMAGE

Emily loves her husband Lawrence, but she has a lot of problems with how he presents himself to the world. Lawrence is a building contractor who feels most comfortable in jeans and t-shirts. It's how he dresses for work, and how he dress-

es for play. Lawrence also drives a twenty-year-old BMW "beater" (with a bent front fender) that he is constantly tinkering with to keep it running. Emily knows, intellectually, that these are things Lawrence enjoys, but she has a problem sharing that enjoyment. She doesn't like being seen in his car because she fears she will be judged negatively by friends and colleagues, and she is always bugging him to buy some expensive clothes. Emily feels that she encourages Lawrence to change his image for his own good, but Lawrence is getting worn down by Emily's comments and by what he perceives to be superficial concerns.

Why isn't Emily happy that Lawrence dresses in a way that makes him feel comfortable? Why can't she be happy that Lawrence has a car that brings him such pleasure? At first glance, it appears that Emily has a problem with image issues that makes her very judgmental. But it actually goes deeper than that. Emily also has a problem with separateness that makes it difficult, if not impossible, to separate who she is from who her partner is. If Lawrence is being critically judged, Emily feels critically judged. If Emily *thinks* Lawrence will be critically judged, she anticipates being judged the same way. And in an effort to control that, Emily is constantly trying to shape Lawrence's image into one that she feels is safe from judgment.

Emily needs to learn an important lesson in separateness: Her partner will never be her mirror image. She cannot control that, and the harder she tries the more she will provoke anger and resentment in Lawrence. Emily has to learn to allow for separateness, and to enjoy that separateness. And this work does not start with Lawrence's wardrobe—it starts deep inside of Emily with a process of disconnecting the unhealthy parts of her merger with Lawrence.

Many of us face this same challenge. Whether we like or dislike the picture our partner presents to the world, we have to learn that it is only our *partner's* picture; it does not define who we are. It is much easier to allow for separateness when you can *experience* yourself as separate.

A loving relationship is supposed to be a celebration of individuality in the context of a deep, heartfelt connection.

LEARNING TO TOLERATE—
AND CELEBRATE—DIFFERENCES

One of the hardest things about partnership is learning to tolerate the simple fact that no two people are the same, even if those people love each other madly.

In every partnership, people are going to have their differences. There will be differences in temperament and differences in taste, differences in work ethic and differences in style, differences of opinion and differences in feelings. And that's just the tip of the iceberg. What do we do with all of these healthy differences? Can we experience them as a cause for celebration and an opportunity to expand our own sphere of experience, or does every difference have to feel like a threat?

- If differences make you question your own feelings ("Am I weird? Am I crazy? Am I completely off-base?"), you already know how differences can make you feel insecure.
- If differences make you question your own behavior ("Am I doing something bad? "Am I making a mistake?"), you already know how differences can make you feel judged.
- If differences make you critical and judgmental ("How can you *like* that?" "You're so weird!"), you already know how differences can make you feel superior.
- If differences make you question your own worth ("I must be really dumb.") you already know how differences can make you feel "less-than."
- If differences leave you feeling frustrated and out of control ("Why can't you do this my way?!" "Why can't you be more like me?!"), you already know how differences can make you angry.
- If differences leave you with that awful feeling of "I don't really know you at all," then you already know how differences can make you feel very alone.

Differences stir intense feelings.

More Mantras for Healthy Separateness

Differences between partners can activate deep struggles with envy, low self-esteem, emptiness, control, and fear. And these can't always be washed away with a single sentence. But sometimes the process of coming to terms with differences *begins* with a single sentence, and that's why I am giving you the following list of more "healthy separateness" mantras. When differences surface, using these mantras— repeating them to yourself quietly, again and again—will help you minimize the threatening aspects of differences and allow for a more healthy experience of separateness.

"Being Different, Feeling Different" Mantras:

- "Being different does not make me a bad person."
- "Being different does not make *you* a bad person."
- "Feeling different does not make me a bad person."
- "Feeling different does not make *you* a bad person."
- "Being different does not make me wrong or inferior."
- "Being different does not make *you* wrong or inferior."
- "Feeling different does not make me wrong or inferior."
- "Feeling different does not make *you* wrong or inferior."
- "My opinions are only my opinions."
- "Your opinions are only *your* opinions."
- "My way is not the only way."
- "Being different does not make me less lovable."
- "We can be very different and still be perfect for each other."

HEALTHY SEPARATENESS: WHAT ELSE DOES IT MEAN?

People get very confused and intimidated when they hear the word separateness. What exactly does it mean? How much is too little? How much is too much? What do I have to give? What do I have to give up? Am I doing something wrong? Are my expectations unreasonable? Where do I draw the line? Let's start with some of the common misunderstandings that continue to surround the word "separateness," and then expand our working definition.

Allowing for Separateness Does NOT Mean . . .

• *Eating your feelings.*

When separation is painful, you don't have to hide that reality from your partner. It's important for your partner to know about your vulnerability as long as you're not using that vulnerability in a manipulative way to deny your partner the opportunity for healthy separateness.

• *Living separate lives.*

Having separate closets is one thing; having separate homes in separate states is quite another. Being apart for an afternoon is one thing; being apart for weeks or months at a time is quite another. I would never encourage you to give your partner opportunities to avoid necessary connection.

• *Putting up with unhealthy behavior.*

Supporting his desire to get drunk with his buddies every Friday is *not* allowing for healthy separateness. Neither is supporting her desire to spend every Saturday afternoon with her ex-boyfriend. You should never feel obligated to support or encourage destructive behavior.

• *Allowing for noncommunication.*

There is a big difference between being separate and being silent. I would never encourage you to give your partner opportunities to avoid necessary conversations that foster meaningful connection.

• *Growing apart.*

Allowing for healthy separateness encourages the growth of the couple *as* a couple, while acknowledging and allowing for healthy and important individual differences. It is not a mechanism for driving a wedge between you and your partner; it's your way of saying, "For us to grow as a couple, we must also grow as individuals."

Allowing for Separateness DOES Mean . . .

• *Giving up control.*

A healthy, loving partnership can't be controlled. You can't control your partner's behavior. You can't control your partner's desires. You can't control your partner's feelings. The only thing you *can* control is your contribution to the partnership—*i.e.*, your willingness to work.

• *Giving yourself permission to be separate.*

Allow yourself to be separate, and give yourself permission to be different. Don't keep the focus on your partner—your partner isn't the only one with needs for separateness. Whether or not you are ready to acknowledge it, you have those needs too. Stand up for your own separateness.

• *Taking time to take care of yourself.*

You are not an asset to your partnership when you're not taking good care of yourself. Don't make sacrifices that are self-destructive. The recipe for partnership requires *two* healthy individuals.

• *Learning To Be Alone.*

We don't enter into a loving relationship thinking about being alone, but when you cannot be alone, every separation is a threat. Being a strong, healthy partner is a lot easier when you are comfortable with yourself. Separateness shouldn't feel like a painful void.

Allow for Separateness

• *Allowing your partner to be a whole person.*

Don't fall into the classic trap of trying to make your partner look, feel, act, or think more like you. Don't censor or discourage those aspects you don't feel comfortable with or don't understand. Your partner needs to feel completely welcome—foibles, flaws, and all.

• *Allowing yourself to be human.*

You are not expected to be a perfect clone of your partner. You are a human being with human differences, and these differences add to the relationship.

• *Learning to trust.*

Healthy separateness doesn't make two hearts disconnect. The connection holds; often, it grows stronger. If you are clinging fiercely to your partner, you can't know that. You will only discover it when you find the courage to let go and allow for separateness.

CONCLUSION

The path to loving partnership is something that most of us seek. Yet it is also something that is so easy to lose track of, take for granted, neglect, or even miss entirely. *Relationship and partnership are not one and the same thing*, and this is something I cannot emphasize enough. A relationship begins when we find a partner, but partnership does not begin until we can *act* like a true partner, and our partner reciprocates. This is where the nine secrets I have presented in this book become so important.

The "nine essential secrets" facilitate partnership—they are nine different roads that all lead to only one place: the place where hearts are joined. Relationships will always be challenging. But relationships do not have to be hard every single moment of every single day. Having a good set of instructions makes a big difference. Yes, you have to work hard. Everyone has to work hard. But when the process of building a relationship starts to make sense, and stops feeling arbitrary or accidental, the "work" takes on a very different feeling. You don't feel lost, at the mercy of the universe, and you don't feel that you are wasting your time. Decisions are easier to make. Results are more predictable. And your love has a sense of direction and purpose. You don't have to put all of your faith in magic and miracles. And that is a really big deal.

My goal in this book has been to make the path to loving, lasting, effective partnership more obvious, and to make your transition from relationship to true partnership more simple. Integrating these nine secrets into the day-to-day workings of your relationship should not be an overwhelming chore. Even if these secrets are not completely intuitive or obvious, there is something very simple and basic about each

THIS IS HOW LOVE WORKS

one. And even if the language is completely new to you, the ideas behind that language are probably somewhere "in your bones" already. These may be the guidelines you have been waiting for, but what makes them so easy to accept and integrate into your life is the seeds that have been planted through your own relationship experience.

Whether they recognize it or not, the most successful couples I know are always working to integrate these nine essential secrets into their thinking and their behavior. You can look for shortcuts, or you can try to "wing it" and blaze your own trail, but the connection you are hoping for may founder. These guidelines are not a "quick fix," and they are not something you want to rush out and start following just because I, or anybody else, say they are vital. These are guidelines you want to fully understand, fully feel, and fully live because you *know* they are vital. That takes a little more time, but it also leads to permanent changes in your relationship. You don't need to "master" all nine in one day, and you shouldn't try. This is a book about day-by-day process and day-by-day practice. Learning about partnership is also a process. So take your time, enjoy that process, learn from your mistakes, and let this material slowly become part of your most natural instincts.

Being somewhat of an independent spirit myself, I know how hard it can be sometimes to embrace the advice of others, no matter how well-intentioned that advice is. I can only say, in response to this, that embracing the advice and experience of others and their practice of these nine secrets for loving have given me the partnership I have always hoped for—a partnership that continues to grow and strengthen. In this book I have written what I have learned. Now it's your turn. There is no reason you cannot have the partnership *you* have always hoped for. Let these secrets lead you there.